Stay Safe and Well

Well

MOM, ME, AND HER OCD

Dr. Juliane Giordano

This book is for all the children raised by parents with OCD.

Contents

INTRODUCTION

Meet The Parents

"Because there's nothing more comforting than someone who actually gets it. Really gets it. Because they've been to the same hell as you have and can verify you've not made it up."
—Holly Bourne, *Am I Normal Yet?*

When I was a teenager I joked that Mom was neurotic, Dad was psychotic, and I was both. I thought I was playing with words but I suppose I wasn't playing at all. Neurosis and psychosis were the air we breathed in our home and thus permeated the cellular makeup of my siblings and me. I saw myself in both of them, in Mom's anxiety and fears and in Dad's short temper and self-aggrandizing ego. My family's influence is a big part of my story, of how it began and evolved. This introduction is the foundation to understanding the roots of my journey.

My parents, Vincent and Angela, were good people, great in many ways in fact. They provided a home for us and were loving, caring, and kind. Many times it was just an ordinary day in an ordinary life with ordinary parents...from the outside. To dig deeper beneath the surface however, would be to discover the authentic artifacts of our real story.

Mom and Dad had their flaws, as we all do, but with the added bonus of mental illness. To diagnose my own parents, as a clinician, is a never-ending endeavor and one I eventually had to surrender. I couldn't always see the storm from inside the eye. What I have best been able to identify is that while most obviously and undeniably Mom has Obsessive-Compulsive Disorder, it is merely the crown to the others. She is a mixed bag of co-morbidities of depression, anxiety, PTSD, and personality disorders, of which narcissism is most likely. But just as the diagnostic dictionary of mental illness lacks precise criteria, Mom and Dad fail to fall into neat categories. Dad's core issue was likely PTSD from a childhood worthy of comparison to Angela's Ashes, with a homicidal father and a cold, critical mother. He had intermittent rage disorder, bipolar tendencies such as intense emotional volatility, aggression, agitation, grandiosity, and a personality disorder characterized by traits such as narcissism.

These clinical labels don't speak to who Mom and Dad were but rather how they were. Beneath their illnesses and defenses they had big hearts, each in their own way. Mom's love was very ethereal, the kind that floats high in the air, never quite reaching the ground…where we were. She was idealistic in what love represented, like fairy-tale delusions. Love was snow-tipped peaks above a burning fireplace, a Hallmark movie in December. Men were meant to carry their women across thresholds of reality, into a place of eternal innocence and reverence. Love had no place for anything contrasted to the snow-white depiction of childhood fantasy, no dark places of tension, conflicts, or even passion. She could only live a life appropriate for a G-rated audience.

Dad loved to be center stage. He sang like Frank Sinatra. I wish I would have appreciated it then, instead of shrinking at the restaurant table, as he would randomly break out into song. Nearby patrons swooned in contrast to my shock and horror. He was Liberace in Robert DeNiro's body. Dad was an odd combination of romance and terror, effeminate emotionality beneath a tyrant's rage. He tried in vain to hide tears in dark theaters, but his chest shook in its cage. I was uncomfortable sitting next to him as he wept, as I often was around his emotions. He was overly demonstrative, a touchy-feely, Italian American with too much intensity and not enough boundaries. He felt entitled to slap "his" women's butts and stroke their faces. He would come up from behind, and give full body embraces that made every inch of my own body brace with apprehension. As his heart melted in love for his daughters, ours guarded up like fortresses.

I shared this with my therapist at the time and she coached me on how to communicate my needs to him. I had been down this path before, carrying the well-intentioned advice of others. It took a lifetime of disappointments to finally stop taking recommendations and give up the fight.

But I heeded one last time. Dad and I sat with our feet dangling in the pool. I was thirty years old and the host in my Scottsdale home. It was a one-on-one opportunity that I saw fit for such a conversation, so I ventured into the realm of hope, again.

"You know Dad, I really need to ask something of you," I began, in deference.

"Anything," he said, putting his large hand over mine, which was sandwiched and invisible, between his and the hot pavement.

"Well," words lumped in my throat.

He glanced at me sideways, inviting me to continue.

"It's just that now that I'm older, I just feel, like maybe, the way you touch me, well, makes me feel uncomfortable."

He gazed out into the distance taking time to consider my request, as the hum of the pool filter ground loudly in my ears.

Tightening my hand beneath his he finally said, "I'm sorry I just can't. I love you so much, I have to show you, and I just can't."

I felt the muscles in my back contract and the tips of my sweaty fingers tingle, pressed into the brick surface. I wiggled them free of his suffocation and said, "Well, Dad if you want to show me your love you can respect my boundaries as a woman. I am old enough to set the rules for myself and this is what I am needing. I'm not asking as much as I am telling you." He sat for a moment as if to take in the words, and a sliver of hope dangled in the air.

"Here's the problem Juliane," he said, like a doctor giving bad news, "my biggest problem is my ego. It always has been. It's just how it is. I am not going to stop showing you my love, I just can't. I'm sorry."

I glared at him with as much disgust as disappointment. We could have gone back into the house together, shared lunch and a cold drink after a swim in the Arizona summer heat, but instead, I got up and left him there, and never went back.

When I was a child I was wild like a weed, with about as much concern for aesthetics and purpose. Life was a moment by moment endeavor of sun in my face and wind in my hair, a puppy in an open car window. I endured school until I could go outside. I couldn't wait for that recess bell to finally ring. I rushed home to make the neighborhood races that met up at the Cunningham's front yard, the starting point from where we'd take off at the count of three. We stood back-to-back, like Hamilton and Burr, jetting off in opposite directions around the block back to the finish line from which we had started. I took off with all my might, hoping...no...needing to finish, more than even needing to win. It was something I had to prove to myself, to know that I was worthy, and not only able to compete, but to complete. Halfway through the race, I was always grabbed by that dreaded side cramp, but quitting wasn't an option and after I rounded toward the finish line, I'd arrive breathless, in an astonishing victory. I wish Dad had been there to see any of those times when I had proudly come in first, but he wasn't.

What he did see was what I didn't want seen, especially all the times I had quit. The clarinet lessons, the Girl Scouts, the...nope, that was it. Just the two was enough to designate me as the quitter, *always* starting things I didn't finish and costing him money time and time again, only for me to give up. I was a wasted investment.

How Dad saw me meant everything to me. He depicted a leader in every way, strong and demanding, assertive and arrogant. When he was in my corner, I shined my brightest. And when he tore me down, I spiraled into the darkest of places. He was my hero and my nemesis, my protector and my threatener, my supporter and my oppressor. I idolized him and abhorred him. We were the most alike in the family, and as is often the case, we sparred with our own reflections, forging a love/hate relationship. He hated the things he saw in me that were like him, and I did the same for him. He detested my impulsivity and emotionality, I his need for attention and validation. We were of the same mold and yet we never came together.

Dad and I also shared a common anger in not having Mom. We wanted and needed her and dared to express our hurt openly. We were demanding of her love and, although repeatedly rejected, we kept hope alive in the chase. For her, we never stopped fighting. I don't think Mom ever wanted to give herself up to anyone. She had more important things to do and a life that would never merge with ours. She lived internally, in her own world, coming out to visit only on occasion. She looked after our necessities, food, clothing and the like, and committed to keeping us safe and well. As long as we were clean and breathing, she was good. All those other inconvenient needs, were frivolous and a waste of time. She soothed our emotions as a child would a doll, patting our faces with a "there there". As outwardly loving as it appeared, it failed to reach those painful places that required understanding and guidance. It wasn't her fault though, she couldn't teach what she hadn't been taught, or emulate what she hadn't witnessed. She did her best, but it wasn't enough. So she shamed me for needing more than she was able to give and was burdened by my tireless need for her attention. She wasn't a bad mother, I was a bad child, and I accepted that as our truth.

Mom's compulsions come first, like a drink to a drunk. She is so glaringly chained to her disorder, and yet she cannot admit this to herself, so this too is our fault. If not for us she would be free from her imprisonment of never-ending days and nights of cleaning. She sterilizes every inch of the house, for us. She washes curtains when she is out of clothes to clean, for us. She checks the pilot light three times, to keep us safe. She scrubs the toilet daily, and when she runs out of things to sanitize she goes upstairs to clean her sister and brother-in-law's toilet, for us. It's all for us and because of us. If only she had become a nun like she wanted she would be free from all of it, and us.

Dad and I competed with Mom's OCD. We needed Mom to be better and we needed her to see us. We were unlike my siblings in that way. My brother, ten years my senior, seemed not to care much one way or the other. He put our family's problems in his peripheral view and went on with his life with as much distance as he could. His battle was more internal, as ours was external. We warred not just on the inside but with each other. He was above that, in his perspective. I suppose he figured a battle that wasn't winnable wasn't worthy. Instead, he buried his head in the sand and his heart in the murk. He closed up and off from us. I don't think he realized until well into adulthood the price he paid for looking the other way, at the times when he lay on the sofa laughing at Johnny Carson as Dad raged at my sister in the next room, my brother practicing his manufactured immunity to my screaming pleas and Mom's thump upon the adjacent wall as Dad pushed her aside. I know those repressed scars remain for him, as the echo of his laughter remains for me.

His brotherly advice was to ignore Dad, to ignore all of our problems. Don't let them get to you, he'd say, and move out as soon you're able. Unlike him, who was allowed to go off to college at eighteen on a full ride, moving out would not be an option for me. Of course I wanted to run away like he did, but beyond not being able, I felt compelled to stay and fight for better. I took on our dysfunction like it was my doing. I needed to show us all that I wasn't the person my parents made me out to be and they weren't the innocents they portrayed. I fought for exposure to our underground reality, to bring our family story conscious. I didn't know that at the time, too young to understand my role, but I can see it today.

16

Although my brother was the intellectual of the family and the most well regarded as such, I could no more take his advice and ignore what was going on in our home than I could endure a nail drilled through my heart. I brought an unwelcome focus to our many dysfunctions and as the youngest in the family, my insights were repeatedly dismissed, flicked away like fleas. My brother once professed that I hold onto the past whereas he and my sister live in the now. We have switched roles in our later years. He woke up at sixty to realize his grudges had grown painful layers of moss. His anxiety has led to more than one ER visit. His doctor offered an anxiety diagnosis incognito, hyper adrenaline disorder, as my brother is intolerant to any psychological vulnerability. He is nearly seventy years old now and angry at things that happened when he was six. He blames and demonizes our father for his suffering, withholding forgiveness and an opportunity at his own healing.

My sister, five years my senior and the middle child, tries to balance it all. She oscillates between my brother's way of coping and mine, from passivity and avoidance to hurt and anger. She carries the additional weight of childhood sexual abuse, perpetrated close to home but outside our immediate family, and her emotional volatility is tenfold. Her feelings are heightened by trauma and she is often unable to regulate her reactions. The fighting between her and my parents was often dramatic and traumatic. She pushed the boundaries, was disobedient and obstinate. She was fearless in the face of our father's rages, provoking him like suicide by cop. Witnessing those incidents were traumatic for me as well. They terrified me in a way that should have terrified her but didn't.

My sister, perhaps, needed Mom more than any of us and she didn't have an understanding of her own neglect. She believed our parents to be absolute and beyond reproach because that's what we had been conditioned to believe. She drank the Kool-Aid and, despite her acting out, she loved our parents beyond the capacity of my brother and me. Mom's blinders hurt her, as they hurt us all, betraying her need for protection and safety from the outside predators she was victim to while Mom was busy with her OCD compulsions. Like Mom, my sister uses passivity now to achieve peace— harmony at any price—in her adult life. But while passivity goes down quite easily, even achieving a short-lived peace, it will sooner or later begin to rot your gut.

My life's mission has been to keep the rot from taking residence in my own body. Cleaning out the psychological toxins and planting healing seeds is a daily routine essential to my own well-being. A lifetime of work in psychology has been like a spiral staircase, at times feeling like I'm not making progress, despite going higher with each step. We don't ever truly get there, not like the monks and prophets, but we can achieve enough peace through facing our stories and their underlying truths.

Someone asked me the other day what I thought of the mental health of our nation over the last four years. What I talked about is what a lot of clinicians are seeing right now, which is a national psychosis caused by the degree of misinformation and rejection of fact, science, and truth. Truth is the foundation of our sanity, without which we are delusional beings living twisted and distorted lives. When our sense of reality is pushed underground we become doubtful, rageful, and disoriented, the very seeds of mental unrest.

This book depicts my journey in my own truth, the truth of my family as I experienced them, and experiences that helped shape and define me. I encourage everyone to identify their own stories and narratives so as to never lose their own truths, which will evolve as new information becomes conscious and larger realities emerge. The integrated whole of our experience reveals itself in the process of peeling back the layers and seeing what's there, updating old storylines, beliefs, and influences, and piecing the broken vase back together, into a more beautifully imperfect perfection.

While my family dynamic is complex (as most are), my mother's OCD was the fulcrum on which we all teetered. I write this book, as a therapist and adult child of an OCD parent, with a dual purpose. The first is to offer my own story, so as to give the reader a true understanding of the experience from a deeply personal and honest perspective. It is my hope that others who have had similar experiences will finally get their long-awaited validation, as OCD is a disorder that is commonly overlooked and underestimated in terms of its severity and impact. There lacks a true understanding about the complexities of OCD symptoms and the suffering those symptoms can cause—symptoms that more often provoke jokes instead of empathy or compassion. We tease people for organizing their desks, or ourselves when we can't get that pot clean enough, "Sorry, I'm in OCD mode." We kick it around like a casual illness, three simple letters that comically abbreviate our eccentricities. Consequently, this has caused a kind of public inoculation in terms of appreciating OCD as a serious disorder. This, despite a 2016 study that reported suicidal ideation was found in more than half of OCD patients in the study group, and that sixteen percent had a history of an actual attempt.

The second purpose of writing this book is to offer the reader ways in which they can heal from the effects of OCD parenting, as well as the impacts of parenting with any type of mental illness, on both psyche and soul. As adults it is critical that we see our experience through the lens of education and understanding so that we may finally realize that while we have been adopted into a world of irrationality, we can now identify for ourselves our own truths.

Further, we can separate from the compulsions themselves and realize that we are not them and they are not us. We are not the mess to be cleaned or the burden of the parent but rather innocent victims of this complex disorder. We are not bad, dirty, or wrong, nor are we the causes of depression and anxiety. If we feel unworthy, we can build insight into the hows and whys and remodel our sense of self.

The consequences of OCD parenting are complicated and painful and, unlike other mental illnesses such as depression, addiction, bipolar, and schizophrenia, there is not enough information available to help families navigate this maze. Until recently there was an appreciable absence of published research or treatment modalities targeted toward children of OCD parents. At the time of this writing, there are a few places that offer family member support but not nearly enough to answer the needs of so many. It is estimated that there are between two and three million American adults with OCD which means the number of children thereby affected is staggering. This is a bewildering black hole in mental health outreach. I was excited to find two recent doctoral dissertations on the subject as well as a handful of blogs. It's a start. The International OCD Foundation is a useful resource for OCD sufferers and their recent article acknowledged the lack of information available for children of OCD parents and the need for family intervention and support. You can find more information on their website https://iocdf.org.

Children impacted by any type of mental illness are worthy of attention and help, and while each child's story is unique, they also share many commonalities. Anxiety, confusion, and poor self-esteem are typical consequences of unstable parenting in general, not solely due to specific diagnostic illnesses or even any illness per se. There can be many causes of instability such as unmanaged grief, trauma, and crisis for example. But regardless of the cause, the results can be unfortunately similar, and while this book is motivated by a need for information about OCD in particular, its applicability is much farther reaching. Anyone who was raised by an emotionally and/or psychologically unavailable parent will relate to this story, as well as to its recommendations for healing.

CHAPTER 1
Genesis

"In every moment, the Universe is whispering to you"
—Denise Linn

There's a thing about words. Sometimes they hold a place in your psyche like a bookmark. A client of mine once explained that she fell in love with her husband before she ever met him. His name on a company roster just held her attention a beat too long. She was inexplicably smitten by the sound of it and knew in a moment they would be together someday. That was how the word "counselor" affected me. I had a general understanding of the word but its meaning was less relevant than its allure, which demanded my attention like a spell. Like my client, I too fell in love with letters on a page. "Counselor," I'd repeat silently like a refrain, a wonderful resonant melody.

I am a believer in synchronicity and pre-determined fates and think coincidences are underrated. I believe people are pulled into certain circumstances and drawn into living lives they were meant to live. And I also believe that ultimately we possess free will and have the choice to heed the calls or resist and, depending upon our choices, we either live harmonious or conflicted lives. The path is peaceful, its detours distressing.

To get a sense of how powerful coincidences can be one only has to look to the Minnesota Twin Study. Researchers conducted a twenty year in-depth study of 137 pairs of twins raised apart, as a comparison group to those raised together, in hopes of understanding how human behaviors are motivated and influenced, and to delve deeper into the Nature vs. Nurture argument. Is it our genetics that make us who we are or our environments and upbringing? An article published in 1980 in the Smithsonian about the "Jim Twins" made for some fantastical reading. Jim Lewis and Jim Springer are twins who were separated at birth by adoption, and reunited at thirty-nine years old. Neither was aware of the other's whereabouts and one of the brothers had been told his twin was dead. When they finally met as adults, they were shocked to discover similarities almost too incredible to be true. Both had been named James by their adoptive parents, both had married twice; first to women named Linda and second to women named Betty and both had sons named James Allan (one spelled James Alan). Both had, at one time, a dog named Toy, driven light blue Chevy's, and worked as Sheriff's deputies. The men were astounded, as were the researchers.

While one can reasonably argue the merits of random coincidences one can't dismiss the countless unexplained phenomena like the Jim Twins. My years of studying psychology have repeatedly circled back to the concept of synchronicity, an alternate understanding of coincidence that assigns meaning to a random world.

When my client told the story of her fated husband-to-be I felt her pang of excitement, reminiscent of how the word "counselor" ignited my interest like the Fourth of July. My passion for psychology has existed at my core for as long as I can remember, and likely before. It is no less a part of me than my arms and legs, and no less essential. I feel compelled to share with you how my inner counselor first showed herself to me as a child, so that you can get a glimpse into how a tiny seed manifested into a fully blossomed reality.

It's 1972, we are ten years old and alone in my basement. Ryan is a slender boy with red hair and cheeks. He was the Robin to my Batman, the Tonto to my Lone Ranger and he never tired of shadowing my ego. He once made me a red leather wallet in the shape of a heart, stitched together with shiny black vinyl rope and while impressed by his craftsmanship I was sadly immune to his puppy love. It's not that I didn't want to return his affection, I liked him a lot. It's just that sidekicks didn't kiss in the movies, they had each other's back and when one's heart got broken the other was there to pick up the pieces, they were for the mending not the breaking.

Eventually Ryan moved on when a friend of mine became the new object of his affection, which made me secretly crazed. But until then he persevered. "Want to play doctor?" he asked me in a whisper. I had to pause for a moment to ponder the meaning of his question.

"Sure." I said, opening the drawer to my father's desk, fumbling through its contents. Ryan looked at me perplexed, his eyes questioning.

"A notebook and pen." I said rifling though Dad's pilfered office supplies.

"Why do we need those?"

"To take notes."

"Notes? You're going to take notes?" he laughed.

"What's so funny about that?" I asked, hurt in my voice. "That's how they do it." Silent and puzzled Ryan simply stared at me.

"That's how doctors do it." I clarified, "I ask you questions about your feelings, then you answer them and I take notes, that's how it works." Finally a look of understanding flashed over his face. And then his shoulders dropped.

"So," I flipped open my notebook, "let's start with your Mom."

"What about her?" He asked in defense.

We were entering a completely different rabbit hole than the one he had hoped for and his disappointment quickly turned into agitation.

"Well, tell me how you feel about her".

I am not sure where I had learned the questions, where

I might have heard them before. I was likely channeling Dr. Hartley from The Bob Newhart Show who had intrigued me, even at ten years old. He was the yin to my father's yang and his deadpan reactions to madness left me laughing and hopeful.

We were sitting across from each other, me sitting behind Dad's enormous mahogany desk and Ryan on the opposite side looking equally shrunken in Dad's king-like leather chair. I continued my barrage of questions, as though a secret trove of material inside my head suddenly escaped. I asked how he felt at school and on the playground when the other kids used his lunchbox for a game of Salugi, a kind of monkey-in-the-middle game meant to taunt weaker kids. I wanted to know what it was like for him, what he thought and feared, what he believed, what he didn't want people to know. And just as he always had, he accepted his default position, this time the Charlie Brown to my Lucy Van Pelt.

"My mother hates me." He said it fast like ripping off the band aid and the moment the wound hit the air, giant tears spill onto his flannel shirt. "I think she wishes she never had me."

His honesty jolted me, I felt thrown, and I felt my face flush. The lid of Pandora's box was open wide, sharp teeth exposed. Doubt took over, shaming me for my careless exploration. I had no response. What should I say now? What if he has a real breakdown, then what? I had heard about those, people who went suddenly mad and wound up in institutions with wires on their heads. My aunt was one of them. I had sat many hours in the waiting room while she told a stranger of her darkness, behind a closed door. I'd sit imagining what demons she possessed that once had her come at my father with a steak knife as I tried to shield him with my body. Whatever her psychiatrist did in that office seemed to help, to morph her agitation into stillness. Like the mighty Oz behind the curtain, he seemed to magically fix her problems.

Sitting with Ryan now, it wasn't that I shied from his emotions, I preferred those to the silence that alternated with the chaos of my own home. But sitting so close to his pain made me desperate to fix it. I felt paralyzed, my mind locked in neutral. Blankness filled my head but for one single thought, "What have I done?" My mind refused to offer a wise response, or at least an empty platitude to ease my own discomfort. I could only sit still, helpless as my friend's sorrow evolved into a weeping mess, pre-adolescent snot wiped across his freckled cheeks. Maybe, I considered, there were no words to be found, maybe that was the point. As his sobbing reached a crescendo, the need to fix what I couldn't possibly dissipated from a stab to an ache, and in that moment it stopped being about me and my fears but rather about him and his broken heart. I felt both a merging and a distancing, as incongruent bookends, as though each was needed to balance what was between them. Come close, but not so close as to eclipse. I noticed as my face began to mime his, mirroring his sad eyes, crescent mooned lips, pointing down to his chest. Our bodies seemed in synch, like two currents running through the same wire, connected to the same source. As we waited out the storm of our young unbridled pain we seemed stronger in unity, a more resilient being created by two separate spheres of experience.

This experience with Ryan would become the genesis of my therapeutic process, what I now understand to be the standing witness, and what a powerful gift a listening heart can be if fully attuned, present, and connected. Although wanting more than anything to "do something" rather than be in that pain with him, I had no choice but to sit and simply feel. I wanted to debate his beliefs and feelings, to convince him he was wrong about not being loved, but wouldn't that just make him feel worse…and wrong? Just as it did when my father told me not to be afraid of that bee that just landed on my cheekbone. Really? Don't be afraid? Fear isn't the natural response here? I think not Dad. Sure, my stomach felt sick from being so close and yet so helpless, but my young experience and instincts beckoned me away from the tempting wave of the wand, ordering me not to fix it. So often we want to stop the suffering so that we can return to our own "ignorance is bliss" existence, failing to realize that by doing so we add to the pain with invalidation.

I don't know if I genuinely helped Ryan that day but I'd like to believe that by being seen, known, and accepted by someone who loved him helped him to accept his own darkness with compassion. The truth was his mother, of course, loved him but she did a great deal to hurt him as well, and her intermittent disgust for him was palpable at times. We all saw it. To deny that reality and convince him otherwise would have only fractured his relationship to his own experiences and truth, as well as contributed to his beaten down self-esteem. By allowing the pain in, we honored his right to feel it while validating what he saw and knew to be real. My experience with my own mother taught me the importance of accepting and authenticating the truth whatever the cost because when we question what we experience we unconsciously reject and disown our perceptions. The majority of my life I believed what I felt and experienced was wrong because I did not have the right to my feelings. I wasn't allowed to be upset, that was an adult privilege and the further I got from my feelings the harder it was to know and have a relationship with them.

As therapists we all want to heal the world's pain, a patient at a time. A mentor set me straight early on stating bluntly, "It's not your job to make the patient feel better." I didn't know what to do with that, it floored me. Then what the hell is my job? I thought, utterly bewildered. The answer was larger than I imagined. It was to be a catalyst to their individuation, to help them find the way back to their authentic Self, which is often anything but pain free. It's hard to fight that urge to rescue the Ryans of the world but in doing so we offer an alternative to fostering a dependency upon us, and rather a way for the patient to become their own hero.

We never know for sure if our memories are entirely real or partly hatched and, like all humans, my memories include my own fill-ins. Our brains can't tolerate missing pieces so it provides stuffing to even out the lumps. So this could be my own filler here, but I recall something shifting in me that day with Ryan in my basement. It was perhaps my first glimpse into the human psyche. By allowing me to explore his pain with him, making space for both of us to hold his feelings, together, safe from ridicule and rejection, my experience with Ryan yielded for me an opening of my heart, and a feeling of love for another person's pain. I had discovered compassion. I believe this was the very experience that would forever drive me forward in this field, and that I had taken the first step in what would become a lifelong journey. I will forever be grateful to Ryan for allowing me into his world and gifting me with an invaluable self-discovery.

CHAPTER 2
A Starless Sea

"A beach is no place to put a school, it's trickery."
—Unknown

It wasn't until high school that I would have my own counseling experience, when I'd become a fixture in my guidance counselor's office. It was in 1976 that I began my tenure at St. Bernadette High School, an all-girl Catholic school an hour's bus ride from my home in Rosedale, New York. It was a school I never expected to attend but rather a default as I hadn't been accepted where I had hoped and hadn't a backup. My best friend jumped on the opportunity and gave me her best sales pitch to join her at St. Bernadette and I reluctantly acquiesced despite it seeming like a strict and oppressive environment. It was vastly different from my Catholic grade school, which had been uniquely progressive and where the nuns wore street clothes and were kind. At St. Bernadette's they ruled with humiliation and fear, which are two of the worst learning conditions I would come to find out.

The social environment at St. B's was also unlike my grammar school. Instead of the rare clique, the girls there grouped like inmates, forming blocs of power via affiliation. There were the Howard Beach, Ozone Park, Brooklyn, and Rosedale clans. Although Rosedale had always been my home, I lacked any connection to this particular group of girls who were a mix of brainiacs and ruffians, neither of which I felt drawn to. As freshmen we had heard the legends, tales to keep us in place, like the story of the Howard Beach girl who gossiped unwisely about one of the seniors and had her hoop earring ripped right through her lobe. It was a visual deeply branded into my memory. I didn't think it possible to split an ear in two and shuddered at the thought. If one assumes that an all-girl school is a safer, less aggressive environment my experience poses otherwise.

The first day of school snuck up quickly after a summer spent questioning my decision. Something in my gut knew this wasn't the right place for me but there was no going back. The thing I dreaded most was having to make new friends. This required a confidence I had lost, like one loses that thing you didn't know you were missing until you go looking for it.

I wanted to go with my friends to the public school nearby but Mom said it had gotten too violent since my sister and brother graduated and that I was too mouthy not to get into a fight. It was another example of her not really knowing me. I was the last person to get into altercations, afraid of my shadow by that point. Dad had fixed my mouthiness for me, as he had my confidence.

On the morning of my first day, I put on my uniform and nervously awaited my new journey. The bus picked up just two of us at our stop, and I immediately swung into the seat next to my friend. From the moment I sat down, I felt scrutinizing eyes all around us, and what little comfort I felt in our bubble of two burst on impact. I sat stiffly on the lumpy red leather seat, a small tear scratching against my bare thigh, hesitant to do or say anything that might bring anymore attention to us. My friend, however, was quite excited, eagerly chatting in my ear, blissfully unaware of the surveillance. I recognized the girl sitting across from us from grammar school. She seemed intent on listening to our conversation, not for the sake of joining in but rather for an opportunity to mock. She sneered at my friend's enthusiastic chatter, whispering something to the girl next to her who rolled her eyes. We clearly weren't in my hood anymore, where I was known from the time I could walk and where I was part of the communal family. Even when I'd changed schools in fifth grade, the transition wasn't very difficult as I knew most of the kids from our small town. There were just a handful who seemed eager in ostracizing the more vulnerable kids, marking their targets. The girl sitting across from me on the bus was one of them. She called me a faggot when the term referenced those who weren't cool. This was before we understood what gay was, when the term was a verbal assault of a different kind. When she heard I was dating Bobby, the boy who lived in the house behind ours, she asked him loud enough for me to hear while cringing her face like she had just swallowed manure, "Ew, how could you kiss *her*?" Kathleen Beck would be a thorn in my side for four more years, I agonized to myself, as we bumped our way over endless potholes beneath the El to Rockaway Park.

When we finally arrived after ten or so stops to pick up my new classmates, our bus pulled up to a sea-worn building located on Rockaway Beach. The school stood on the shore like a concrete block, lined with jalousie windows hand cranked open to allow the salted sea breeze in, a marginal relief from a hot, sticky September day. Although relieved to be free from the confines of the bus with Kathleen and crew, I exited reluctantly along with the thirty-five other girls, one-by-one hopping down the rubber clad steps to begin our four years of academic heaven or hell depending upon your intellect and popularity. I wasn't hopeful.

Grouped by the color of our uniform vests, we were clearly marked in red as freshmen and therefore new initiation bait. The rumored traditions were meant to instill hierarchical angst in us, like we didn't already know our standing and shake in our knee-high socks. Gratefully the actual initiation didn't live up to the exaggerated tales. I'm not sure if it was out of self-restraint or lack of creativity, but it amounted to a silly shaming in having us do bunny hops sung to self-disparaging lyrics in lipsticked faces and clothes which, as it turns out, is quite survivable.

On our first day, we were introduced to our assigned guidance counselor who, like us, was new to the school, herself a freshman of sorts. She spoke gently and was visibly eager to meet her first litter of pups. In contrast to everything prior, her presence resonated comfort like a protector in a strange land, cocooning my worst anxieties and doubts. It was a promise of a new relationship. She said her one and only job was to look out for us, and that in her we would always have a friend. She encouraged us to ask for help and assured us we'd always be welcome. Her words sounded too good to be true but I believed them and I believed her.

Ms. M would in fact keep her promises, and like Clark Kent ripping off his glasses, in a flash she was there, always. It didn't matter if I was in a required class hour or lunch break or after school or over the summers or into the late evenings, she was there for me. I found myself gravitating to her office like a force field, without knowing what it was I was looking for, other than to see her face. She had a great face, gently aged with soft laugh lines in accordance with her midthirties, and eyes shining with reassurance. I'd poke my head in, feeling like an interruption, a burden, I had just been there the day before, what could I need again today? But when she saw me shyly peek in her door, she immediately put down her pen, widening the door of her tiny office with her foot, inviting and reassuring. I felt awash in a love light, claimed by a competent adult as I'd never been before.

Our conversations were not memorable and I cannot cite more than one or two. They did not have enough meat to stir the juices of recall. I was the teenager who never talked about her problems, not because I didn't want to but because I didn't know how. I have had many a teenage client since who has sat in my office like I once did, without a substantive story or feeling to share. The chronic shrug of the shoulders will lead most therapists to attempt distractions such as art or music, in hopes their client will open up in the less formal and more creative forum or will at least offer some interpretive material. Ms. M and I didn't engage in those either. Mostly I would simply watch her work, content to be in her company.

As wonderful an ally as Ms. M was to me, teenage jealousy isn't a pretty thing and I felt possessive when it came to my beloved counselor. I hated the sight of her with anyone else, like when I saw Regina, another of the mean girls, making her laugh early one morning. I saw them through the small rectangular window in the cafeteria door, as I ate my snack alone at a long empty table. Regina was flinging her hair about in dramatic pantomime, while Ms. M's smile spread across her face, lines deepening on both sides of her long stretched lips, until Regina's finale made her release a guttural laugh so strong it blew beneath the door smacking my face. I felt small and insignificant, their shared moment eradicating my very existence. My face flushed in anger, I'd never made her laugh like that.

It was one imaginary threat after another, I felt constantly threatened by a competition that didn't exist. Every connection had a fragility, and an anticipated rejection. I hated feeling so vulnerable and insecure, and any attempts to gain reassurance made me feel more exposed. The day that Ms. M heard about my friend Tara's problem was when my jealousy crossed over into a truly ugly place. Tara and I bonded quickly in freshman year, she had a self-deprecating sense of humor that made me feel at ease. You never feared embarrassing yourself with her because she always beat you to it. I valued her friendship and thought I'd do anything for her if she ever needed. She had become my best friend at St. Bernadette. But when word about Tara's drunk father abusing her reached Ms. M I discovered exactly what kind of friend I was. Ms. M came to the door of our algebra class, interrupting Ms. Perry's chalking of x's and y's, and asked to see Tara in her office. I could see in her eyes that whatever was going on with Tara was serious. I felt both worry and jealousy, a curdling combination that made me want to vomit. When Ms. Perry instructed Tara to go with Ms. M, she reluctantly got out of her seat, head down and eyes averted. She looked like she was walking toward the guillotine, which I couldn't understand. How could anyone not want to go with Ms. M? Didn't she know that having her attention was the best thing in our pathetic teenage lives?

I sat staring at Tara's empty seat, feeling disgust in my pitiful envy, in place of what should have been empathy for someone I thought I cared about. How could I be jealous of someone else's pain, to ache for a wound that would make Ms. M tend to me like that? What kind of person was I to feel this way? Like Mom said ad nauseam, "Why wasn't anything ever enough?" I didn't understand the existence of contrary feelings yet, believing one feeling must blot out the opposing, rather than both being true. I couldn't possibly feel both love and resentment, that didn't make sense.

I wished I was able to ask for the things I couldn't name. It would take years into adulthood to finally identify the source of my insistent cravings and yet still I couldn't ask for help. My wounds confused me, and I vacillated between feeling overly sensitive and overly justified. I didn't know where my pain stood in comparison to others as though a comparison was relative. I compared my father's abuse to that of Tara's and came up short. I didn't have a measure for other sources of pain until later, when I would learn that it was a longing for my mother's love that left me feeling emptier than I could ever rate or articulate.

Emotional neglect is hard to talk about because there isn't anything to point to, it's the absence of something. It's like seeking the unseeable. As neglected children we don't know what we don't know and not getting our basic emotional needs met is something even adults struggle to put into words. In fact, neglect is so destructive that it causes more dysfunction in children than even abuse. Human beings can handle horrendous adversity more than they can handle not being seen.

I was jealous of Tara because she had a name for her problem. It made absolute sense, it was clear and known and reasonable. Of course she was in pain, there was an obvious cause that anyone could understand and because it made sense, she made sense. I, on the other hand, made no sense at all. My demons were ghostlike, like swatting away invisible bees I feared I simply looked crazy. Worse, Tara gave Ms. M something to work with and talk about in some meaningful way, which meant they shared something I could not. I assumed in those deeply personal and vulnerable talks a connection was had that I would never experience.

Spending hours watching Ms. M work at her desk, sitting in an adjacent chair, smoking her cigarettes, skipping class after class was a temporary fix, an escape that failed to yield any lasting confidence. While appeasing my chronic need for her and getting me through high school, our time together amounted to a momentary respite from my insecurities. I usually left with the same problems I had come in with. Maybe if I had given her the opportunity like Tara had, I too would be feeling better and getting better grades. But instead of feeling better I was often left with an abrupt and painful withdrawal from what was becoming a highly addictive drug.

From a clinical perspective, we develop what is called object permanence as babies. By the time we are eight months old we have learned that when someone leaves the room they haven't disappeared forever and will be back. In secure attachment we can feel that presence whether the person is with us or not. However, in insecure attachment we struggle with feeling connected when away from the loved one. Instead of experiencing an anchoring when apart, we often feel untethered, empty, and alone. The bliss of feeling safely connected is only a prelude to the inevitable jolt of separation.

Early misattunement is one of the causes of insecure attachment. When a baby cries and the mother mirrors the baby's discomfort the baby feels seen and a relationship to his

41

or her needs begins to develop. Mom sees me therefore I am. If Mom fails to mirror the baby whether in misreading the cues or an indifference to them, the baby will fail to develop trust and learn to dismiss their needs as irrelevant. Mirroring comes in the form of copying the baby's expressions, when baby smiles Mom smiles, when baby frowns Mom frowns. Mom feels what baby feels. When Mom soothes the baby from a place of attunement, the baby is soothed and begins to build trust in their environment.

My own mother had wonderful and loving intentions but thought that laughing in response to a baby's cry was helpful. While patting our mouths as we screamed, turning our wails into the Native American hand-over-mouth war cry mockery kids did in the day, she wrongly assumed we'd be entertained and distracted from our pain.

Today we know better. In a video of the Still Face Experiment by Dr. Edward Tronick (http://www.youtube.com/watch?v=apzXGEbZht0), a mother is seen playing with her baby as the baby sits in their highchair, the baby in obvious delight in the positive interaction they share. But then suddenly Mom stills her expression, no longer smiling or reacting at all to her baby's gleeful coos. In a matter of moments the baby grows increasingly agitated and begins crying in anguish as the mother is no longer mirroring or responding to them. The degree of distress in not getting Mom's smile is heart-wrenching to watch. Depressed parents often meet their baby's gaze with similar flatness, unknowingly and unintentionally affecting the baby's sense of well-being. All parents have incidents of this happening of course, however, it is the chronic or acute cases that more often result in a disruption in the attachment process and create deep rooted insecurities in the child.

We each have actual mirroring neurons in our brains that activate feelings like empathy and altruism, necessary emotions for our social survival and evolution. Without connection, there is no community, without community there is no safety. In a threatening world our tribal instincts are critical. When we can feel another's experience we will connect and support each other. The mirroring between mother and infant is perhaps the most critical as it begins in the earliest months of our development. Without secure bonding we risk narcissistic self-survival and sociopathology.

My mother was too ill with her disorder to prioritize my needs as an infant. She was often preoccupied and too impatient to see what I really needed and when she did see, her needs often trumped mine. In psychology we refer to the "good enough mother" as a measure of adequate care. Pediatrician and psychoanalyst Donald Winnicott posited that perfect parenting is actually detrimental to a child's well-being, in that small frustrations help the baby to increase their tolerance in not getting immediate gratification. It is a careful balance, however, of what is too much and what is too little, what is too early in their development and what is too late. The good enough mother meets all the baby's needs at first and then gradually decreases her availability, never more than a couple of minutes, however.

My work in learning to trust relationships has been long and difficult and there were times when I wondered if I would ever feel safe anywhere in the world. Luckily, the brain is very adaptable and positive experiences create new and more efficient neural connections. It's never too late for the brain to change. Ms. M was, for me, the mirroring mother I needed, fourteen years into my development. She saw me so I was seeable. She loved me so I was lovable. My needs mattered to her and that alone paved the way. It would be a long road in its building but in time I learned that my use to others was only as good as I was able to get my own needs met. Self-nourishment is essential and not selfish. My challenge is that my needs seemingly fly above my head and outside of my radar and constantly need to be lassoed in, which requires a lot of conscious awareness and checking in with myself.

Chapter 3
Girl Interrupted

"I told her once I wasn't good at anything. She told me
survival is a talent." —Girl Interrupted, Susanna Kaysen

My relationship with Ms. M faded after graduation. We spoke on the phone but after a while it just all seemed pointless. She had new students to save and my face would be replaced by a fresh one. I felt anxious and alone in what was expected of me now that I had a diploma. I tried to envision a future but I didn't know what to wish for, I saw only a dark road without any street signs. I don't know what dinner table conversations my friends were having with their parents about their plans after graduation, but our table was silent on the topic. Neither of my parents had the proper insight into me as an individual, or an understanding of what was important to me. To make a valid assessment of where I would excel, their help would have been like taking a personality test for a stranger.

Gaining insight into the needs of a child cannot occur when the mere mention of needs is extinguished like a threat. Sharing my problems was met with a shaming rejection, as I was often judged as needy and spoiled. Dad came from the school of "never pick up a crying baby" and that philosophy held over the years. He detested the idea of a needy child so it was best to teach the child how to buck up on their own. He rarely bothered with our troubles, and even speaking of them made him angry and disgusted. A man who had spent his childhood abused in ways depicted in horror stories, had become intolerant of our privileged discomforts and while he was committed to the avoidance of such pain for his own family, he grew to resent us for it. The thing about trying *not* to be something is that paradoxically you become that very thing. My father in many ways became like his own father, whom he held in hateful contempt.

We often attempt to correct our legacies by becoming their opposites but either way you bend the coin it still won't work in the machine. Like how they teach you in drivers ed to avoid looking directly at the pedestrians and keep them in your peripheral view instead, as we are apt to steer into the object of focus.

With Mom, our problems were an intrusion of her very busy schedule. "There's just not enough time" she'd reiterate again and again. There were more important things than our needs. There were her needs, which were always triaged first, although in Mom's narrative her life was a never-ending parade of sacrifices. I never thought to question that claim. The answers would have exposed a very startling reality, albeit one she never would have accepted. As I saw it, it was she, not we, who needed us to be scrubbed, sterilized, and perfect.

These were not sacrifices she made for us, that kept her from living a bigger and better life. They were obsessive needs that precluded us from a more innocent and carefree childhood. A true sacrifice would have been dealing with the discomfort of not heeding a compulsive call, in favor of our well-being.

In a strange contradiction, my parents were overly permissive in the most critical things, such as alcohol, drugs, sex, and such, to which they always looked the other way. The only things that ever required what my father deemed discipline, and what I deemed his self-indulgent temper tantrum, was disrespect. The things we did outside of the house weren't their concern, if they didn't have to see it, it didn't trouble them. But sometimes the things we did outside brought the problem inside, like my sister's hickey, which the world could see and judge. It was okay to be out there playing around with boys, but she made the mistake of bringing it home.

I always thought myself prematurely emancipated, on my own earlier than nature intended. I knew a sense of longing well before I knew the alphabet. I yearned for guidance and, although fiercely wanting independence, I knew beneath my punky kid persona that ten-year-olds shouldn't be making decisions about smoking, drinking, and necking. I have nasty memories of picking up smoldering cigarette butts off city streets to smoke (take that Mom's OCD!); sneaking a thermos of my aunt's best scotch up the block for me and my friend to drink, sitting on the curb quite satisfied with our act of piracy, albeit spitting out most of it; and my boyfriend attempting second base in the basement when my mother unexpectedly came down to do the laundry. She was more embarrassed in catching us than I was in being caught, and her deadly silence afterward was her typical reaction to anything uncomfortable. I wanted to be reigned in, I begged for it in my insidious acting out, but nothing ever came, only the blood curdling yells about cookie crumbs found on the kitchen floor. That was intolerable.

I didn't want to be doing the things I was doing, they made me feel bad about myself. I took to writing daily pledges in my journal, promising the great beyond that I would stop doing x, y, and z. I believed that whatever it was out there that existed, did in fact care about me, but was also very displeased. I held guilt in my body, emotional weights that slouched my shoulders in an attempt at invisibility. I had a curvature of my spine which caused constant back pain. "Stand up straight" my father would bark, pulling my shoulder back in a Mr. Spock death grip. I'd obey but in minutes it was in a slump again, my backbone holding the brunt of my shame. I was told I mumbled and was instructed to practice talking with a pencil between my teeth. Then the bouts of stomach pains followed, and the dreaded Irritable Bowel Syndrome where I would have to race home in need of a bathroom, which was quite embarrassing in adolescence when it was hard to explain why I couldn't wait. I'd hold it for as long as I could at school, ashamed of my body's foul-smelling attacks on me, which naturally make it worse. My friends thought me a drag, often having to cut our time short or cancel plans last minute. I didn't trust going anywhere too far from home for too long in fear of not making it back in time.

Despite my anxiety, I knew I would have to do something with my life post-graduation and when Dad said to choose between work and school, I chose the latter as it was the devil I knew. Maybe a degree in counseling would be fun, perhaps a way of keeping Ms. M in my life in a way, so I browsed the course catalogs and even felt a smidge of excitement. Once again words pulled me in, Sensation and Perception, Human Memory, Motivation and Emotion, Human Development Across the Life Span, Social Behavior, and Personality Theory. I was curious about all those topics and even held hope of healing myself, or at the very least understanding my problems. I couldn't silence the curious monkey on my back who was insistent on answers, wanting to know why I was the way I was, did the things I did, or what caused me to feel what I felt. I believed everything had a cause and I needed to know what they were. Maybe these classes would help to answer some of my questions.

I wanted to go to college out of state, Colorado in particular where one of my aunts lived. I'd always loved the West, and felt it was a place I could breathe. But it was not to be. I was eighteen years old and my father was a child of the Great Depression. He was practical, and psychology was hardly that. Further, he and my mother thought leaving home a ridiculous idea, although my brother was admired for going away to Cornell. While my father strived toward an egalitarian philosophy about gender, at the end of the day it was simply idealism.

Dad wanted me to do something he could both be proud of and keep me financially secure. Not a crazy ideal for a parent, at least not on the surface, yet I hadn't given him much to work with. My high school transcript had only one shining star and that was in accounting. I wasn't especially good in numbers but the sociopathic Sister Agnes had me fearing failing more than death. I managed an A, which Dad held onto like a dog with a bone. "Accounting" he said, would be my major. His deciding my scholastic future was not open for debate.

When the schedule for my first semester at St. John's University came in the mail, there were new provocative words that jumped off the page at me: Macro Economics, Micro Economics, Western Civilization, and Business Statistics! Terror replaced intrigue, as accounting replaced counseling. Each day, in each class, I sat in the very back of the room attempting to hide my glaring ineptitude. While everyone else seemed to be following along, all I heard was a cacophony of foreign verbiage. I felt completely disoriented and lost. Attention Deficit Disorder wasn't a thing in 1980 but it was a reality in my brain. I had always struggled with staying focused in school but in areas of disinterest it was nearly impossible. Teachers were constantly saying things like "doesn't use her full potential," and "she can do better if she applied herself." It meant nothing to me hearing those assessments. They were obviously unaware of the countless hours spent crying at the kitchen table as my brother tried to make me understand algebra. I would yell at him, throwing my books across the table at the torment of what could only be my utter stupidity.

The constant haze of confusion at St. John's caused terrible self-doubt and confirmed those earlier assumptions. There had to be something lacking in me and yet I also sensed something bigger was untapped and trapped behind a padlocked gate. I knew I could do better, just as the nuns had said. I just couldn't *do* better. I felt exposed at St. John's, always on the precipice of the next humiliation. I vacillated between feeling too seen and not seen enough. I was often disoriented and frequently got lost on the vast and intimidating campus with thirty-two buildings and ten parking lots. It was the rare occasion that I found my car on the first attempt, often walking a frantic mile, feeling like the foolish freshman I was. The lots packed us in like sardines and I'd have to maneuver around cars haphazardly parked halfway up the dividers. At times I'd struggle getting out of the space, parked so tightly I often came home with sample streaks of paint on my car door. Each day began and ended in stress.

It was a dense cloud in which I lived, foggy minded and fatigued. The most insignificant endeavors were exhausting. When I came home I'd retreat into my bedroom, lying on a bed that felt increasingly smaller and less comfortable by the day. It was a restless kind of fatigue, a jitteriness that I was too drained to relieve. Worse was the feeling of not being real in my life, as though the world outside was busy with normal people doing their normal things and living their normal lives while I existed in the atmospheric layer above, an untethered wraith.

When I explain the experience of depersonalization to my patients I can see the relief come over them. I understand the solace in identifying our unnamed experiences. Most people who have had the sensations of depersonalization feel as though they are going insane and in simply knowing their experience, while immensely uncomfortable, is neither life-threatening nor proof of their insanity, is therapy in itself. For all my years with Ms. M we never spoke of anxiety and its many scary faces. I wish I would have known then what I teach my patients now, but there is healing in giving a gift one never got.

Depersonalization is a little-known symptom of panic attacks, and a form of disassociation. It can make the sufferer feel as though they are looking at the world from inside a glass bubble, not being a part of it but rather outside and detached. In my experience there were moments when I would suddenly realize I was away, off in a kind of daydream, only a much deeper place. Some people describe it as a trance-like state. The first time it happened I was fifteen years old and sitting in a classroom when I awoke to the realization that I had missed a good part of the lecture. The blackboard seemed unusually far away but too close at the same time, and my body felt as though it was being lifted out of the chair while also falling down onto the ground. I was in a crazy land of opposites, nonsensical and upside down, I was Alice in the rabbit hole. When I raised my hand to go to the bathroom, it didn't look real floating above my body. I stumbled my way into the hallway like a drunk, my legs feeling not my own. I couldn't imagine what was happening to me and was afraid to tell anyone. This was shortly after I'd had a bad experience with marijuana. I'd had a horrible trip and completely lost connection to my surroundings. I'd gotten physically sick, vomiting relentlessly for hours. I went in and out of a dream-like dissociative state, unable to coordinate movements or function. For days I was trapped in a nightmare, one minute feeling fine, the next like I was being sucked into a black hole again. Avoiding my parents, I didn't even know what it was that I was hiding. I closeted up and avoided everyone. Thankfully, in a few weeks time the episodes began to lessen, coming less frequently, but the mere thought of them would be enough to trigger their onset.

Although never officially diagnosed, I was likely experiencing flashbacks from the pot I had smoked, which was likely laced, as the weed in the 70's was infamous for trippy concoctions. Just to double down on the price of my poor decisions, the flashbacks had since become the basis of all my anxiety attacks. Still today they arise on cue, I only have to think of them, only now I understand how to manage them and they don't last more than a moment or so. Most times.

As a side note, researchers have found that cannabis use can cause the onset of panic disorders, anxiety, dissociative disorders, and even psychosis. Just in case you're thinking of starting now that it's legal in many states.

CHAPTER 4
The Best Wallflower I Can Be

"I got my own back." —*Maya Angelou*

Eventually my anxiety developed into agoraphobia where I feared leaving the house. I began to fear the fear, feeling anxiety about going anywhere I might have a panic attack. In the classroom I would sit by the door in case I had to leave abruptly. Large open places like shopping malls felt too large, like there was no place to ground myself. Driving was the ultimate threat, fearing I would lose control of the car. I stopped going to school, or going anywhere. It quickly became a horribly small existence as I sat in my room day after day, refusing to leave or talk to anyone. I couldn't eat, and breathing was an exhausting chore. The last memory I have of being at St. John's was of standing at the top of a concrete stairwell looking down and seeing myself plunge to the bottom in a free fall, not intentionally but inevitably. I had had enough, Dad's disappointment would have to take a backseat, his threats no longer holding weight against what I was experiencing. The charade at St. John's would have to end, and to his credit he ultimately decided that a life of poverty for his youngest child was just a tad bit better than one of insanity.

Without anyone to help fish me off the bottom, I was completely alone. The days of hiding out in Ms. M's office were long gone. Months went by in slow motion, my body felt aged and leadened. Mom and Dad seemed to resent the space I took up in their house and their brains. They worried about me but did not have the ability or interest to know my pain. They simply wished either it or I would go away. There was a secret growing inside me, bigger than my academic misery and I suspect they suspected it as well. I was changing as my sexuality started nudging toward the surface. It would poke its head and I would beat it down. It terrorized me. It was 1980 and not a good time to be gay. There were no role models, no representations, no places to meet people other than creepy bars. I sent away for a list of contacts in hopes I could meet a single person like me. I paid ninety dollars, nearly $300 today and an absolute ransom for me at the time, and awaited the mail delivery in shameful anticipation. I felt perverse at my core. When the list arrived I panned through the names, crushed in not finding one person in the same state, remarkable given New York City's reputation as the deviancy capital of the world. I kept the list in its stealth envelope for thirty years as a reminder of just how dark those days were.

One night Mom entered my offensively dated bedroom, with red carpet and childishly pink curtains that frilled at the ends, to say good night. We talked about my going to

Colorado to visit my aunt for a while. We agreed it might be good for me to get some fresh air and a change of scenery. She asked if I wanted to take a friend, maybe a boyfriend. I told her I had given up on boys, at which her brows met in a pinch. She paused for a long moment, weighing the possibilities in her mind and finally said, "You're not trying to tell me, God forbid, that you're gay?" There's only one answer to a question asked in that way, and I gave it to her. Denial on a silver platter, dinner for one.

I did go to Colorado for a while, alone, and it did help. I felt the weight lift off my achey body and the mountain air made it easier to think clearly. I decided I needed to figure out my problems on my own and that I would do it by learning. I could do for myself what I needed from Ms. M and wouldn't need her or anyone else for that matter. I began by reading every book I could find on panic disorder and learned its complete physiology. I started to see anxiety in a new way, less of an enemy to be battled and more with curiosity. I learned to identify exactly what was happening in my body, which allowed me to be less fearful and more confident in my ability to defuse it. I learned that my reaction to my panic was the most important thing to work with and that if I could tolerate and even befriend the fear I could successfully manage it.

I used the relaxation response and diaphragmatic breathing when stressed and checked in with my body more often, scanning for tension and negative and irrational thoughts. I actively countered my stress with internal supportive coaching, "You will be fine, you're not really dying, it just feels that way. This will pass. It always does. You're okay." Sometimes the coaching was soft and patient, like Ms. M, other times firmer and more assertive like my father. Just like children, our inner states need flexible communication. When a three-year-old heads toward the hot iron we need to be tougher and Dad's commanding demeanor had an efficiency in certain arenas. I was learning to tap into that. Sometimes we have to truly believe in the "no" in order to set the boundary properly. If I disciplined myself with the expectation of disobedience that's what I got. When I lovingly told myself "Enough!" to the irrational, self-demonizing chatter, I meant it and I felt its intention to protect versus shame me. I expected my psyche to listen and it did.

In time I began expanding my world, taking more risks and pursuing new things. I felt a renewed energy and desire for life and didn't fear Dad's rejection like I had. Many things in my life got reprioritized as they do when people face their own mortality, even a psycho-spiritual one. I felt as though I had survived the mythical hero's journey down in the underworld and returned to the surface with the boon, which was a sense of self. I enrolled in community college, despite Dad's condescending brow. "So what are you going to do with that degree?" he asked. "I want to go on to be a psychologist" I said. "No, you don't," he corrected, "you want to be a psychiatrist and hang a shingle, like a real doctor." I had no interest in shingle-hanging and in fact wanted to be the best wallflower I could be. I preferred being out of the limelight, more background than foreground. Foreground always felt like a threat and it was where my father lived. His ego demanded grandiosity and I preferred the shadows of such. I didn't need to impress anyone, I just wanted a respite from my anxiety and maybe even a touch of happiness.

My two years at community college were as wonderful as St. John's had been wretched. The course curriculum was a melodic recitation of Child Development, Human Sexuality, Anatomy and Physiology, Sociology, Abnormal Psychology, Any-ology…sweet Jesus, oh my! I loved my textbooks, which were filled with information like that of my research on panic attacks. Learning about human behavior helped me to understand my own family and relationships. I read books like "The Drama of the Gifted Child" by Alice Miller, which turned a light on the darkest of things. It is an amazing book that affirms childhood experience and validates the suffering caused in our early years. I felt freed from the anchor of self-blame. The high schooler who barely read a dozen books in her life, was now an insatiable reader. The loneliness I had felt in the years before melted in the sunlight of knowledge.

In my second year, I interned at an Alcoholics Anonymous group, which required attending daily meetings, one of which was for gay addicts. I was overwhelmed by the number of gay people in one room as I hadn't met a single out person in my nineteen years aside from the crazy looking woman who worked for my father and who wore a leather cuff on her arm with steel spikes jutting out at me. If that was gay I wasn't sure I was up for the transformation. But in this AA meeting there weren't any horrifying ensembles to be found and in fact most attendees seemed pretty normal. The exposure to people who were living openly in their sexuality was profound for me. Like a kid from the backcountry let loose in the big city, I was both excited and terrified. Looking back it is hard to fathom that growing up in Queens, New York encapsulated so much small town thinking, but that was how it was.

I fell in love with the 12-step program immediately, drawn to its structure. It is essentially a road map for healing and it offered me a method to explore my problems in a way that felt organized versus overwhelming. I worked with one of the group members who taught me how to proceed through the steps and I eagerly threw myself into the work. I also met a lot of lesbians.

My two years at community college concluded with graduating with honors. It marked a time in my life in which I had finally found a part of myself that felt authentically me. Finally I was successful at something and I was happy. Even Dad was proud.

I intended to pursue the next step in the journey toward counseling but as the Yiddish saying goes "if you want to give God a good laugh tell Him your plans." Family tensions had grown to a point that I had to reposition my course. The night I decided to leave home was the night my father attempted to break down my bedroom door. It was over yet another ridiculously overblown offense, this time not respectfully saying good night after a day of arguing with my mother. As he screamed threats and pounded his fist against the hollow door, I sat on my bed numb. My family's experience with Dad's violence was old and tiresome. His intermittent rage was a thing you can both count on and not predict. Sometimes he'd go off the handle if I was a minute late, other nights he'd barely notice me stumbling in drunk. Turning the key in the door was a crap shoot. I had hoped that as we both got older things would change, he would mellow and I'd gain some freedom and independence but after seeing him throw my twenty-five-year-old brother across the kitchen table I had to be realistic.

I applied for work at a temp agency the next day, and was sent to interview at a major financial institution. I didn't want an office job even though I wasn't quite sure what it would entail. What the position of collector was I didn't know but the temp agency said it was the only job they had that didn't require experience. In the interview I answered the questions with the worst possible answers. I said I didn't like working on the phone, sitting at a desk, or working on a computer. I hadn't been coached to interview and although it should have been obvious to me, at the time it was not. I thought I was supposed to answer the questions honestly. Who knew? The interviewer just smiled at me and made some notes. The next day I got a call, I got the job. That's how bad of a job it was. No one wanted it, so why not hire the kid who admitted it.

I loathed the position but showed up robotically each day. It was quite like my Catholic high school experience with managers who used shame and humiliation to keep us in line. The department manager was a five-foot militant woman with short white hair slicked to the side. She unapologetically kept a bottle of scotch in her desk and drilled us daily on our productivity. One day she caught me on a personal call and banged my desk with her fist. Berating me in front of my peers, she grabbed the phone from my hand and slammed it into its cradle. With a red face I sat stunned. "Get to work," she demanded as she turned on her orthopedic heels.

The salary was enough to rent a room on Long Island. I answered an ad to share a railroad style apartment which consisted of a long hallway with four tiny bedrooms branching off its main, a single bathroom and living area to share. It was above a store on the main shopping street in Malverne, a quaint town next to the railroad tracks. For the holidays the street lit up like Bedford Falls and I immediately fell in love. Although only a few minutes from my hometown, it felt a million miles away.

I had promised myself to leave the night Dad banged on my door, and now just a few weeks later, I was on the precipice of a new life. I was fearful of his reaction, unsure if he would bully me into staying, but I was determined to leave one way or the other. I sat on the news for a few days, working up the courage and when I finally made my big announcement he didn't believe me. "I'm moving out." I blurted. "Sure," he said, "you can't even clean your room never mind live on your own, where are you going to get the money for that anyway?" With that I held up the key as evidence and his eyes went from surprise to rage. I was twenty-one years old, clearly adult enough to leave, yet for them it was an unimaginable betrayal. How could I do such a thing, they wanted to know. I had stopped caring about their feelings long ago, just as they had mine. I was intent on taking care of myself despite the pain I was seemingly inflicting on them with my selfish act of independence. "I'm going," I persisted, "and you have to respect that." He stood towering over me uncharacteristically speechless.

Under their silent glares, I packed the small amount of belongings I was allowed to take. It was Christmas Eve, we didn't speak. I asked Mom to pass me the albums as I packed a small U-Haul box. She said she wanted no part of my decision and walked out of the room. I left without goodbyes and spent our family's favorite holiday with a stranger and a bottle of wine in my new communal living room. It was sad and scary and it was stupendous. I had never been on my own and the freedom was invigorating. What would I do? I had no idea but I was eager to find out.

I had to learn so much on the spot as it was. I had no life skills, as Dad so kindly pointed out. I didn't know how to balance a checkbook (despite that A in accounting), apply for credit, obtain insurance, cook anything other than eggs, or budget my spending. My first grocery shopping outing was a mortifying experience, having to put back half my order as the cashier gave me her best condescending smirk, but humiliation is a strong motivator and the next time she rang up my groceries I had more than enough to silence her judgment.

I worked as a collector for the next six years. Six very, very, long years. I applied for supervisory jobs and was never considered. I watched as coworkers who seemed not particularly skilled get promotions instead of me. I couldn't figure out the equation. I personalized it, with the "there must be something wrong with me" demon returning and the more I questioned my value the worse I performed. I wound up leaving the bank, getting jobs with their competitors, another bank, a collection agency, an attorneys office. Then four years later I returned. My significant other at the time was in management, the same woman who interviewed me back in my "I don't like phones" days. She vouched for me as I applied, and with her help I secured a supervisory position...sometimes you need a rabbi, albeit an Irish one. The second time around I was relieved to discover new skills. I managed people well, understanding and utilizing the relationship between validation and motivation. I worked well on a team. I could forecast numbers from an intuitive versus mathematical basis and while I didn't love the work it was far better than being on the phones.

Over the next few years I unenthusiastically climbed the corporate ladder. I chased the next rung simply because there was one. We all did. We followed the bait like hungry fish, not caring what the next promotion entailed but rather the status associated with it. We were trained to work cooperatively, but also competitively. There was an undertow of cutthroat mentality. We exchanged smiles in meetings and yanked the rug from beneath each others' feet behind closed doors. Those who rang their own bells excelled the most, but as women we had to learn to do it with deference. The lessons were plentiful.

I learned two critical life lessons during those years. The first is if anyone ever tells you that the squeaky wheel gets the grease don't believe them, unless what they mean by grease is hardship, then do. Complaining about most things only gets your own flaws noticed, and using your energy toward a negative outcome will work against you in the long run. I had a boss who was undoubtably corrupt if not criminally, certainly psychologically. He was a masterful manipulator, brilliant in his games. In my attempt to right his wrongs, I sounded like that dreadful squeaky wheel, and instead of putting a spotlight on him, I found one on myself, and instead of him losing his job, I lost mine. Shortly after I was gone, he was fired. When I was no longer there to distract from his offenses, the spotlight defaulted to him and he was left holding the accountability bag for all to see. The universe has a much better way of sorting out injustices and, while we need to advocate for the more vulnerable as well as ourselves, there is a point at which we need to step back and let all the variables work themselves out. Of course there are critical exceptions but in most instances we need patience as each of us has a necessary path to travel.

The second lesson was that if you fail to take the path you are meant to take your unconscious will do it for you. I hadn't enough faith and motivation to leave my job, particularly once succeeding in promotions and earning a decent salary. I had grown comfortable in my discomfort, repressing my grief at a lifeless career. I felt there was too much to give up in leaving and certainly no one really liked their job anyway, it's just something we all have to do. That was the mindset of many people at that time. Work was a means to an end, not something one found fulfilling. At least not where I came from.

Self-sabotage was something I learned growing up. If I shot myself in the foot Dad couldn't force me down his chosen path. I did not have a voice, or any control in my fate, so destroying my own potential seemed like the only way out. I didn't do it intentionally or consciously but reflexively and mindlessly.

Getting myself fired from my very lucrative job took some doing. Although I'd often wanted to quit I never gave it real consideration. However, my unconscious mind was setting up an escape plan for me, expertly destroying every bit of my success, bringing it all down brick by brick and ending in a dramatic finale. It had found for me, a way out the door, through which I was pushed like last week's garbage.

During my unemployed hiatus I made the decision not to return to the corporate world. Feeling I had nothing to lose I enrolled back into school to finish what I had started ten years prior, to get my counseling degree. I was thirty-three years old and Dad still discredited my decision, warning me that I would close a short window of opportunity as employers don't like gaps in resumes, "You're not getting any younger," he reminded. I assured him I knew at this point in my life what I wanted and didn't want and that I'd survive the mediocre pay. He wasn't convinced. I didn't care.

From that point forward I never looked back. The journey this time was uninterrupted and completely my own. Like it had been at community college so many years prior, school was once again a high for me, learning, a drug. I was excited about the long drive to campus where I met others who shared my passion, with whom I fit in easily. It was a natural path, everything came easily, including good grades, and the road felt smooth and clear. When we are on the right track it's like that. Everything just flows. I had finally arrived at the home within myself.

CHAPTER 5

Life on the Bottom Rungs:
When a parent is too busy

"What people somehow forgot to mention when we were children was that we need to make messes in order to find out who we are and why we are here." —Anne Lamott, Bird by Bird: Some Instructions on Writing and Life

OCD is classified as an anxiety disorder. Symptoms include recurrent obsessions or compulsions that are recognized as excessive or unreasonable, causing significant distress. Patients will often spend hours a day preoccupied with these thoughts or behaviors that interfere with normal functioning and relationships. According to the New England OCD Institute, there are four subgroups of OCD and symptoms may include some or all of the following: 1) Contamination and Washing, 2) Doubts About Accidental Harm and Checking, 3) Symmetry, Arranging, Counting, and Just Right OCD, and 4) Unacceptable Taboo Thoughts and Mental Rituals.

The American Psychiatric Association defines OCD as the presence of obsessions, compulsions, or both. Obsessions are defined as:

(1) Recurrent and persistent thoughts, urges, or images that are experienced, at some time during the disturbance, as intrusive and unwanted, and cause marked anxiety and distress.

(2) The person attempts to suppress or ignore such thoughts, impulses, or images or to neutralize them with some other thought or action.

Compulsions are defined as:

(1) Repetitive behaviors (e.g., hand washing, ordering, checking) or mental acts (e.g., praying, counting, repeating words silently) in response to an obsession or according to rules that must be applied rigidly.

(2) The behaviors or mental acts are aimed at preventing or reducing distress or preventing some dreaded event or situation; however, these behaviors or mental acts either are not connected in a way that could realistically neutralize or prevent whatever they are meant to address, or they are clearly excessive.

Mom had most of the symptoms listed. She wasn't especially concerned with having orderly canned goods like the stalker in the movie *Sleeping with the Enemy* but obsessed as much on washing, cleaning, worrying, and checking. She also wasn't a hoarder but rather the opposite in throwing absolutely everything away. I don't have any mementos from childhood, not a game, a dress, a doll, a picture from the fridge. Everything is gone. Mom couldn't handle clutter, even the kind stored behind old metal closet doors in the basement. The less we had the less apt to get dirty or, worse, become a hiding spot for bugs.

The older I get the more I miss the ability to look back upon my childhood memories. As a young adult it hadn't occurred to me that I would someday miss the blue vinyl barbie doll case that contained years of fantasy play, or the Dancerina doll that twirled when you pressed down on her pink crown. Today's toys feel sterile in comparison to the clumsy technology of the day. But the content of my memories felt like a burdensome mess for Mom, far less important than the joyful experiences they represented. As my client anguishes over her inability to throw away a single picture her five-year-old daughter has drawn since her hand was able to hold a crayon, I am struck by the disparity of experience. What must it feel like to be loved in that way, I wonder?

The OCD diagnostic criteria stated in the DSM-5, the diagnostic reference book for clinicians, doesn't take into account the impact on others or on relationships. My personal stories would come as a surprise to most people, even clinicians. The diagnosis fails to consider just how far reaching the illness is in terms of its trickle-down effect. This is sadly reminiscent of when my mother-in-law had major brain surgery and the world-class surgeon told us that if the surgery was successful (which it was) that she may experience some compromises in vision and perhaps in doing math equations etc., but otherwise she'd be "fine." So when this lovely woman became an out-of-control child with constant impulsive and self-gratifying behaviors we were blindsided and completely ill-equipped. The surgeon surely knew that disrupting this part of her brain was likely to alter her personality tenfold, resulting in a heartbreaking inability to maintain relationships with her loved ones. But for most surgeons "alive" equates to "fine" and while she was most certainly alive she was not at all fine.

The criteria for OCD as per the DSM-5 is like that of my mother-in-law's symptomatology, in that it fails to speak to how the symptoms go on to cause relational disturbances, which impact life quality greater than the compulsion itself. It's one thing to be a counter or a checker and another to create an unlivable environment for one's family. There is a diagnosis in the DSM-5 of Obsessive-Compulsive Personality Disorder (OCPD) which does speak to relationship impact, however it is a very different animal. With OCPD a person attempts to control the behaviors of another, is highly demanding, controlling, and is a perfectionist. The negative effects on relationships are obvious. The impact of OCD is more covert. The pain of witnessing the compulsions and the inevitable neglect is more a condition of OCD than OCPD. OCD behaviors don't feel like an aggressive attack on others like OCPD, but rather guerrilla warfare, which makes it far more insidious in terms of identifying its harm to others. In my preteens, we had an above ground pool which I loved. I felt a freedom in swimming and was good at it. For four or five summers I spent long days and even some nights, enveloped in first invigorating then comforting water, as it warmed throughout the summer. I was wholly myself, and experienced my first confidence there. This proved to be fleeting as my mother instructed my father to take it down when the mess of falling leaves and strewn toys and equipment overwhelmed her. Similarly my joy at eating blackberries off the vine was traded away for a clean patio as Mom could not bear the purple stains. These instances are perhaps a little out of the norm but not necessarily outrageous, and this is where the insidiousness comes in.

OCD has become a common moniker for anyone who is particular or perfectionist and there is little hesitation in making jokes when it comes to calling ourselves and others obsessive-compulsive, as though it's a kind of silly personality trait. It is usually met with a laugh of relatedness, a chuckle at our own pseudo-neurosis. Few people think of the brilliant rendition of Melvin by Jack Nicholson in *As Good As It Gets* when making such jokes. The movie painfully portrays the main character's suffering with dark humor, particularly in his ineptness in relationships. Imagining Melvin in charge of the well-being of a child, responsible for his or her emotional, psychological, and spiritual development demonstrates just how incompatible OCD and caretaking can be.

For children raised in OCD households, life can be lonely, confusing, and even maddening. In my own experience I felt like I was the disorder itself. By internalizing my mother's reactions to me, I could not differentiate between me and whatever it was that upset her, I was it and it was me. If she was annoyed at my presence as I interrupted her busyness, I felt like I was a problem. I felt it at my core. My sense of reality yielded to hers, and discerning what was right and what was wrong was simple, she was right and I was wrong, she was clean, I was dirty, she the slave, I the ingrate. That was my reality.

My experience, along with millions of others, should no longer be the norm in today's world, when education and counseling are so readily available. Families can, and should, be better equipped to deal with the challenges of living in an OCD environment via simple outreach. But we have to know who we are reaching out to and if OCD remains in the shadow as the joke rather than the epidemic families will continue to suffer needlessly. While OCD is the fourth most prominent mental illness it continues to be one of the last to get serious attention. This despite its impact on every family member, with children being especially vulnerable. Without an adult's reasoning they are unequipped to handle this very confusing environment. They don't understand why Mom is so upset all the time, why she whispers numbers to herself, or spends hours straightening out the curtain pleats or why she keeps touching knobs like some kind of weird game. But most of all, they don't understand why Mom gets so mad at them when they're just doing what all kids do. Their friend's moms don't yell when a dollop of jelly falls off the spoon and onto the table, so it must be them that are to blame.

Children of OCD parents will often take on their parents' distress and agitation, absorbing them like a sponge. Relentlessly, they try to help the upset parent by being excessively helpful or as much out of the way as possible. They will attempt to check all the OCD boxes, keeping things in order as best a child can, which of course, is unsustainable. Children are made to feel like the burden when in actuality they are the ones carrying the burden. Often, children in these families will attempt to defuse potential triggers in hopes of maintaining harmony in the home, fixing problems before they hit the radar. They grow up prematurely, assuming the role of caretaker and in essence becoming the rational parent, a concept called parentification.

As adults, it is helpful to share these stories with those who have had similar experiences, since while they may seem peculiar to others, for us they were the status quo in living with an OCD parent. Finally we can feel as though our experiences are relatable and from this connection, we can begin to feel validated, credible, and less alone. It is as though something clicks in our psyche when we hear similar experiences and feel a communion with those who have experienced what we have, who have given words to things we have been unable. It's not a new process, as collective story telling is ancient at its roots, from the ancient Greeks, to Native Americans, to AA, to modern men's groups, our psyches seem compelled to tell our stories so that they may repair and heal. I recently found a small bit of research on the effect of OCD parenting and read it eagerly like a whodunit, so deeply curious about what others had reported. Immediately, my sense of aloneness quelled, as though a ghost before, now miraculously seen. My experiences, once thought crazy, were suddenly legitimized, the bees no longer invisible, as I had been swatting at real threats all along. When you grow up around OCD life seems like smoke and mirrors, very little makes sense and you begin to feel as though you are the one who is mad. When I questioned Mom's reasoning as irrational or imaginary I was deemed disrespectful. Our family consistently chose complicity over confrontation, thus Mom was never at fault or ever wrong. Eventually I began to wonder if it was really me who was seeing it all wrong. Maybe I was too sensitive or overreactive as charged. They had nicknamed me Sarah Bernhardt, the overly dramatic actress of their time and maybe the nickname fit, maybe I was overreacting, but sometimes we need to swing that pendulum hard in the opposite direction to find the middle ground. There were times I just could not resist the need to push back at Mom's irrationality and delusions, as it felt like a fight for my own sanity.

In reading the testimonials from other children of OCD parents I saw how both my experiences and reactions were not unreasonable, as I had been groomed to believe, but rather common and necessary. The pain, loss, and anger that result when needs are so grimly overlooked were described repeatedly, in different and yet similar ways. One woman reported how her mother placed a negative value on learning because she didn't want schoolbooks brought into the house! It's hard to imagine how compulsions can eclipse a child's needs so blatantly, and yet there was no shortage of examples.

As adults, interviewees often stated a need for setting strong boundaries with their OCD parent, and having to distance themselves in order to protect their own mental health despite immense feelings of guilt. For me, it was my move almost 2,000 miles away, which felt selfish at the time but I needed to cut myself off emotionally in order to cut the cord. However, like those in the study, I still cared deeply about my OCD parent, and had great love for her as well. My mother's symptoms define her capability rather than her character. She is a wonderful woman, trapped inside a vicious and endless loop in her brain. The fact that she is unable to live outside of her world of compulsions, a world that excludes her own family, does not preclude our loving each other, it just makes it more painful.

Setting limits and boundaries with Mom is difficult to do as our dueling needs are endless, caring for her on one side of the ledger and caring for myself on the other. After fifty-nine years in the making, these patterns of accommodation are highly resistant to change, but it is a work in progress and keeps evolving. I have felt a lifelong obligation to my mother, to take care of her, to protect her, and to be the intermediary between her and the rest of the world. It made the writing of this book very difficult in that it often felt like a betrayal. Telling this story at times felt like a demonization of the woman who raised and loved me with her whole heart. But in fact it is the disorder that I have come to demonize in its hijacking of what could have been and of who my mother was beneath it. It is her OCD to which I attribute tremendous accountability. We suffered together at its doing and without the necessary tools we were its victims.

CHAPTER 6
A Peculiar Bird

"See, I think there are roads that lead us to each other.
But in my family, there were no roads — just underground
tunnels. I think we all got lost in those underground tunnels.
No, not lost. We just lived there." —Benjamin Alire Sáenz,
Last Night I Sang to the Monster

Over the past five decades I've had countless opportunities to analyze Mom and I haven't a shortage of theories. The one that feels most true is that Mom used compulsions to avoid her feelings of shame. But the denial of our darkness doesn't make it go away, it is rather insistent upon expression and will take whatever path is open. This usually comes in the form of projections. We are disgusted by those who represent our shameful repressions and find ourselves hyper-focused on them instead of on our own conflicts. All the insecurity, doubt, and self-hatred gets cast upon this vulnerable target, and acts as a diversion away from ourselves. In the moment it may seem satisfying since it feels better to judge another than to look bravely into the mirror to face our rawest parts. But until we are willing and able to integrate them we will continue to find projections. Swiss psychiatrist Carl Jung stated, "Whatever you repress, whatever you don't recognize in yourself, is nevertheless alive. It is constellated outside of you, it works in your surroundings and influences other people. Of course, you are blissfully unconscious of these effects, but the other people get the noseful."

A neighbor once referred to my mother as a "peculiar bird" and she accepted this with great pride. The neighbor said Mom would rather starve to death than call for help which pleased Mom immensely, "See I never bother people," she would brag, "I'm not one to impose." If you hadn't known my mother you would mistakenly assume her fiercely independent. She was not. She was in reality dreadfully dependent, which for her was a fate worse than death. Mom was foremost concerned with how others perceived her, and to think herself an encumbrance would have been intolerable. It's one thing to be a burden and an entirely different thing to be seen as such.

Mom was afraid of the most basic things in life, such as driving, working, shopping, making phone calls, and generally engaging with the world. She didn't like being bothered with what she called nuisances, as they are interruptions and impositions to her own self-ordered priorities. She was ashamed of her limitations and adept at hiding them in manipulations that effectively got her from A to B. It was a tricky game of twenty-one questions and every need, perceived or real, an exhausting endeavor. Our conversations often went something like this:

"Where would you like to go for dinner?", I ask.

"You know me, I'm easy, wherever you would like to go," she answered.

"Well, what kind of food are you in the mood for?"

"I don't know, you guys can decide, I'll go wherever you like."

"Ok, I'd like Mexican food" (knowing full well she doesn't eat it).

Mom laughs. "Well, not that."

"Ok then what kind of food?"

Mom laughs again, a little less sincere this time. "Any other kind."

"Ok, we love sushi."

There is silence now as Mom is starting to get agitated. I know how to end the game easy enough but some nights I am determined to make her as frustrated as she makes me.

"Vegetarian?" I ask.

"Oh come on Juliane."

"Chinese?"

"No, my sister doesn't really like Chinese food."

Anne lives with Mom as she always has and now sits silently with her in the backseat. She lets Mom do her bidding and wields more invisible power than even Mom, this despite neither of them being tall enough to see over the headrests. They speak with one voice.

"Steak?" I ask, fresh out of poking options.

"Well, we had hamburgers the other day so I'd really rather not do meat again."

"Well," I sigh, "do you have any other suggestions?" A specific choice of words that allows Mom to slip through a loophole.

"Well, okay what about that place we went to last weekend?"

Finally it ends, she wants Italian food as she always does, and will never just say, because she doesn't ask for anything, is easy to please, and never complains.

At dinner Mom is listlessly nudging her food around the plate. "What's wrong?" I inquire, concerned against my own will.

"No, no, nothing, it's fine."

"Do you not like it?"

"No, no. It's just, well, it's tasty?"

"And that's bad?"

"It's just your mother likes things plain," she said, referring to herself in the third person. "I don't like any spices on anything. I don't understand why these restaurants never make the food the same way twice, every time we come it's different."

Mom complains about the food being too mushy, too tough, too "flavorful," too undercooked, too overcooked, too much sauce, too dry, too al dente, and on and on. It has been my life's mission to please her, to make her happy, and to figure out what she needs before even she knows what it is. I was born into the role as she assigned it to me in utero. I would be the answer to her pain and grief and as though encoded in my DNA, I always felt that responsibility. Mom lost her own mother before I was born and beyond the typical grieving, she entered a deeply rooted depression. My parents hadn't planned on more children and in fact, were medically advised against it, but a surprise pregnancy is what would finally give Mom new hope at a time when she had none. I entered the world as my mother's lifeline, and she steeped me in her love and devotion, as though her savior. And as saviors go, my experience would include the sacrifices inherent in the role, in my case being wakened in the middle of the night (she surely knew to never wake a sleeping infant!) to soften her sadness. She loved telling stories of nudging me awake "'Come on Juliane, wake up for your mother', I would sing to you. I just couldn't wait till morning, I'd have to play with you." I have always felt the tethering of that lifeline, to stay awake for Mom, and my responsibility to deliver the nutrients needed to keep her safe and well.

After nearly a century, Mom was still childlike and dependent upon parenting. She was a helpless yet stubborn geriatric, not as endearing as others like to see, but rather infuriating to manage. Beneath her resistance in doing things herself are irrational thoughts and fears that she cannot or will not confront so instead she finds ways in which we will do the work for her without directly asking. By early adulthood I had figured out that the energy spent avoiding and repressing my problems far outweighed the energy required to face them and I refused to understand Mom's way of dealing with hers. In many ways her failures felt selfish and cruel as they were dumped on the rest of us. I had found that burying things was exhausting, and for me, fighting a good fight came naturally. But Mom was different in a way that I deeply resented. Challenges for her were simply not welcome, learning was never a goal, and self improvement a ridiculous concept. Why would she need to do things herself, that's what Dad was for. Her role was to be the master delegator, his her fixer.

Whenever Mom's compulsions arose, she managed us versus them. Our friends weren't warmly welcomed in our house because they interrupted her chores and they were messy. When my best friend came to visit, Mom made a path of paper towels for her to hop from one to the next, my mother following immediately behind gathering the now soiled towels, before landing her butt on the kitchen chair. My friend thought it a game, albeit bizarre. I was mortified. When it came time to leave she looked at me anxiously, not knowing how to hop back out the front door as the paper route was gone. Eventually I stopped inviting friends over because Mom's antics got decreasingly entertaining for them and increasingly embarrassing for me.

As we all are, Mom was complicated. She was both the innocent child and the powerful dictator. Stealth warfare was her typical modus operandi as she only knew how to get what she wanted through the passive-aggressive back door.

Everyone who knew Mom failed to recognize her incredible influence, seeing her as easy going, a follower not a leader, failing to see how she manipulated them to yield to her desires. She was always in charge, they just didn't know it.

Mostly we just wanted to please her. She had the kind of personality where you would throw yourself off a cliff to make her happy, because there is no better thing than her childlike joy. But Mom can also be the three pound Chihuahua who will bite the ankles of a pit bull. Her rage was a simmering cauldron. Silence was her default, rejecting and abandoning with only a glare. She will never hit a child again she said, after her shoe's near miss with my brother's head. But her anger didn't need a prop and in fact, I'd choose the shoe given the choice. Just get it over with.

I used to imagine how it would have been had Mom been better at dealing with her problems, been stronger as a mother. I spent so much time wishing she had advocated for us a fraction as much as she did for her compulsions. I'd find myself needing to escape from those longings by watching TV, shows of the 70's, with badass moms like Annie Romano on One Day at a Time. I fantasized being her third daughter. Her anger was exciting to me, like that of a fierce lioness protecting her cubs. Plus she was cool, a women's libber of all things! How could a mother be a feminist? Yet there it was, the proof right there on the screen. I longed to be part of their family, jealous even of the constant conflicts. At least they were talking to each other about things that mattered, things they felt strongly enough to fight about. Those were the nights though that left me feeling even sadder and hungrier, knowing I was missing something essential yet unnamed.

Mom's refusal to see her obsessions as her problem instead of ours irked me, as did her desire to enlist us into her hellish disorder. If only we'd adhere to her compulsions as she did, it would be her happiest of days. The vision of the five of us spending our lives in the trenches of Lysol and bleach would be her OCD nirvana, even at the cost of our undoing. Except of course the reality beneath the fantasy was that nothing we did would have been good enough and our presence in the midst of her compulsions would have been an intrusion. She said she wanted us there, but she didn't.

Of all Mom's limitations, the one with the most unexpected impact on our relationship was her refusal to drive. Not being able to go out together kept us to the confines of our four walls day in and day out and, although being holed up in her OCD theme park worked just fine for Mom, I wanted nothing more than to be free from it. I wanted to go out shopping like my friends did with their moms, or out to eat at the local luncheonette. These are the opportunities of connection, like couples on date night, a refrain from the routines of mundane tasks and responsibilities or, in our case, a break from Mom's OCD. Any time out of the house was better as Mom was less preoccupied and often lighter, more playful. Despite her social anxieties and agoraphobia she was better when her compulsions were on a break.

Mom could have learned to drive had she just called it what it was. She could have admitted that of course it was her fears that kept her from ever learning, and not the delusional excuses she'd create. Wrapping her avoidance in one of the usual babbling disguises, she'd go on and on, "I never wanted to drive because I didn't want to be bothered taking people here and there. Who needs that hassle, I never had time for such things. I was always too busy, working like a slave everyday for everyone else." This repetitious diversion tired my shoulders, once again weighting us with unimportance. Again, we weren't worthy of Mom's time and energy, our needs reduced to an inconvenient hassle.

Had Mom been honest with herself, she would have admitted, "I am afraid to drive, I can't focus on the road because my head is too full of irrational thoughts and my anxiety would be out of control. God forbid I hit someone or had an accident I'd never forgive myself." Then perhaps we could have helped her, rallying as a family in support and encouragement. She could have exemplified what it's like to face fear and move through the world with courage and determination versus avoidance and denial. Instead of making us feel like a burden in needing her, she would have owned her incapabilities. What's more, we could have related to the fear she felt, none of us having a shortage of our own. That common ground would have put us on the same map, instead of in parallel universes. It would have been gratifying to have an experience we could both understand and talk about but Mom's inability to reflect and communicate her problems disabled the whole relatedness system, instead blowing out the fuse at the slightest charge. At any mention of uncomfortable topics she'd spin out into her OCD babble or bury her head so far into the sand she'd disappear entirely. Instead of turning toward each other in our communal pains we jolted apart like opposing magnets, never finding a place to relate. In place of understanding and compassion, I was left with only anger at her disinterest in dealing with reality. So many times I would ask "wouldn't you feel better if you learned how to do this on your own" to which she'd flatly answer "No." I couldn't understand her thinking, her lack of interest in anything that could develop or strengthen her, it bewildered me. How could anyone not want to feel greater effectiveness, independence, autonomy, and confidence? Why didn't she want these things for herself or for any of us? I couldn't see through the lenses she wore, and it grew to the point that I didn't want to understand because maybe in my empathy my own fire wouldn't ignite, nor a burning to rebel, and maybe if I felt compassion I would not have the justification to want more for myself. I didn't want to be anything like her and although that reality pained me it also propelled me to defy her enlistment. I would never become Mom's protégé, I promised, not ever.

I refused to concede and settle for what Mom had to offer. I provoked her to teach me how to navigate my painful adolescence, to give me a voice and teach me to be a strong woman. I fought against her crippling of my potential by constantly arguing against her absurd logic and found myself wishing her to be my Annie Romano. "Why can't you just stop cleaning and listen to me?", I'd plead. "You're not hearing me, I need you," I'd wail at her. But she would vacantly stare through me. My pleas were alien to her and she simply could not be who and what I needed. Everything I wanted would stay locked behind her disorder, the good enough mother in shackles.

In place of confidence Mom offered me fear, weaponizing her superstitions to dissuade me from trying anything new or challenging. She wasn't interested in things like good grades or hobbies. She cared only about the roller coasters I dared to ride, convinced I'd fall out like she 'almost did,' or my getting lost on the wrong train that would get me killed in a bad neighborhood, as had 'almost happened' to her. Sometimes she'd worry about things she dreamt about or heard on the news. There was no bottom to the pit of her worries. Something was certain to get us and it was her job to keep us alive. Happiness and confidence were acceptable casualties to my safety. A beating heart and breath were her only measures of success.

But it is nearly impossible to feel both safe and fulfilled, and life can feel unworthy of living in a protective bubble. Evolution likely wired us this way to ensure our progress, forcing us out of the cave despite the threats. In the modern world, things like boredom and discontent push us beyond our comfort zones motivating us to live larger lives. But Mom was never bored, infused by her compulsions and worries, she was chronically busy. She did not have any proclivity toward personal growth and while she may have thought that was a personal decision there was nothing personal about it. Parents don't suffer alone, they are the nucleus of the family's well-being. As children we are the electrons orbiting their existence, their wins are our wins and their defeats our defeats.

Mom's failures were scary to me as a child. I didn't feel safe and protected but rather unanchored and vulnerable. She felt far away even when holding my hand. Her energy was constantly frenetic, distracted and preoccupied, in the midst of some unknown quandary. It was internal to her, as all things were. Like a perpetual Rubik's cube being turned over and over again, she was constantly trying to work something out in her mind. Her eyes often glazed over as I spoke, clearly somewhere else in thought. She'd nod her head as though listening, perhaps even grasping the central theme of what I was saying, but without any real comprehension.

I wanted time with Mom that was free of OCD. Time to laugh and be playful. Time to do homework together or watch TV. Time to sit on the porch and watch the world go by. But Mom had two primary coping defenses, doing and dazing. When she was doing the air was thick with tension and irritation as she scurried about with a dust rag, vacuum, or mop, hands gloved in Playtex. Rushing furiously, obsessed with perfection, not one chair out of place, not one crumb at large, not one stain upon her child's shirt could be tolerated.

Everything had to be done in hectic precision. I felt exhausted in her wake. When, and only when, her own exhaustion presided and landed her onto her gold La-Z-Boy recliner had she finally earned her daily pleasure, watching the 4:30 movie classic. I would sit on the floor, cozied up against her legs, entwining into her world like a strand of DNA. I wanted to see what she was seeing, hear what she was hearing, feel what she was feeling. I wanted desperately to know her. In those wondrous moments we would laugh at the old movie plots, Mom beaming as beautiful actresses strutted about confidently in cinch-waisted skirts and pillbox hats. "It was so different then," she would sigh, referring to the lost sophistication of women who dressed with pride "back then." It conjured up images of old black-and-white photos, of Mom tailored in similar fashion, her head tilted toward the camera versus away. I was fascinated by that Mom, who this woman on the recliner had once been, before she became a "slave to this family,"

Our moments of sitting were short-lived and tightly sandwiched between the doing and dazing cycles, and while I treasured them, they left me emptier than before. A taste of Mom starved me for more of her and when her good moods quickly faded, thoughts shifting from the TV to the things that weren't getting done, I felt momentary despair. Our breaking apart left me feeling alone and angry. Why did she have to leave all the time? Dad would be home soon, dinner had to be cooked and the three hour clean up would soon ensue. Mom's free time always spiraled down into the demand of her compulsions and when she answered their call she was gone, like the Three Faces of Eve, disappearing into another personality.

Then there were the dazes. Sometimes I would catch them when she sat at the table alone drinking her tea. Off in space, brows meeting in the middle, as though squinting to see something that wasn't there. Other times they would come on like a seizure and suddenly abduct her, her eyes soft and focused into the beyond. But most often they came when we tried to talk about anything requiring focus or time, topics of complexity or depth. She simply could not maintain her attention. Adrift, she would wander off, into an alternate universe, separate and distant from the one in which the rest of us lived.

CHAPTER 7
A Family Portrait

"You either die a hero or live long enough to see yourself become the villain." —Harvey Dent, The Dark Knight

Our neighbor comparing Mom to a bird is physically fitting, she was like a newborn sparrow not yet ready to fly. Fragile and frail, she was never quite 100 pounds, nor over 5'2" tall. She ratcheted down over the years to 4'10" tall, and vainly trained her doctors to round up in her chart. Dwarfed by osteoporosis that calcified her bones, Mom's back hunched over like a question mark, much to her horror. It was hard to project confidence with a hideous hump following her around. While others may have seen the reality, a simple curving of her spine, she imagined Quasimodo staring back in the mirror.

Hugging Mom revealed her vulnerability, like a sapling, twigs jutting through paper-thin skin. Still she managed to maintain a childlike adorability in her aged body. Strangers smiled at her, like they did puppies and babies, fussing over her and holding doors for her as though the highlight of their day. I trudged alongside her and her sister, delivering them from one appointment to the next, towering over the two miniature dolls walking arm in arm, in matching purses and windbreakers.

Known her whole life as Dolly, she was nicknamed as a baby for her resemblance to a porcelain doll. Her skin still glowed at eighty-eight, barely a crease, splotch, or sag. She sported an old-fashioned coif, teased and abused by layers of lacquer reapplied daily. Her 'girl' at the salon would plead with her to ease up on the VO5, as she picked through the sticky web like unknotting a delicate chain. Dolly was a light golden reddish-blonde, as per the box of L'Oréal, and barely gray even her follicles defied aging. When tenacious black roots returned, once thick and kinky, now more thinned and tame.

Mom's father had stood under five feet tall and they called him little Caesar. Although I lived with him until his death, I don't have a single memory of his voice or a word uttered, only of him sliding the daily mail down the kitchen table as if a puck, toward the net of my bowl of Lucky Charms. This was Grandpa humor, I concluded, as he chuckled retreating back to his apartment upstairs. He would spend his entire morning sitting by the window waiting for the mailman's arrival, and the remainder of his day yelling at the television. A favorite fun fact of Grandpa was the way he 'ate' his meat by chewing it until he consumed all its blood and then spitting the remains into his napkin. When I set the table I placed four folded napkins around his plate, north, south, east and west in a teasing retaliation. And if his eating habits weren't entertainment enough, he wore several watches up his left arm and slicked his hair back with baby oil.

My experience of my maternal grandmother is through stories told by my mother. She died before I was born but Mom has built an image of her in my mind as a woman who glowed in piety. The stories are limitless as Mom has spent her life fixated on her mother, revering her as a saint who never asked for a thing and who never got upset, thus the ultimate martyr. My grandmother, Mom said, enjoyed watching her children from the sofa on which she was confined. We never got a real answer regarding her illness as Mom would always respond to our inquiries with a "she just wasn't a well woman" refrain that seemed to fade into the ether. Mom enters a dreamy haze when she reminisces about her mother, followed by teary eyes and then a spontaneous head jolt to shake the thought out. She says of Grandma that she was the most loving person in the world although not physically affectionate, "She showed us love with her eyes." She was passive and permissive, content being the observer and this is how Mom describes perfection of being—a witness versus a participant in life, as there is no fault with the former and only vulnerability in the latter.

When Mom was a child she was tasked with housekeeping chores at five years old as her mother was unable and her father was busy running his barber shop. As the youngest of five children she was often alone, without companionship or care, and in her loneliness Mom recruited her dolls as companions, giving them baths and washing their clothes. It struck me as odd and sad when she told me this. It wasn't the kind of play I would have hoped for a child. But perhaps Mom was giving her dolls what she herself longed for, love in the verb. Somewhere in her child psyche maybe she knew the roles were backward and that it was her mother who should be caring for her, in the way she was caring for her dolls. Sometimes healing comes from giving what we ourselves need. The dolls made her feel connected, and in giving them the love that was missing in her world she felt less alone. Mom's love for dolls would in fact last her entire life, even into her later years. My father had given Mom a stuffed bear that played "You Are My Sunshine" and at eighty years old she was still pulling the string in its back singing along joyfully, as though the string touched off not just the music but her delight.

Over the course of her life, Mom's chores evolved into fixations, rituals, and compulsions, her deepest relationships with them instead of people, perhaps because they are more reliable in her mind. In reality, her compulsions saved her in a psychological sense from a neglectful environment. I believe Mom's guilt in not being able to fully emulate her canonized mother is at the root of her symptoms. No one could ever be as good as her, "There was just no one like her." No matter the offense, her mother simply didn't react. By comparison Mom's childhood reactivity, or normal child behavior, felt disgraceful, sinful even. The split between good and bad, put all things in either camp, never in any middle ground. Being bad, or even wrong, is not an option for someone with a perfectionistic pathology. They are unable to metabolize any negative thoughts or emotions and thus cut them off like deformed limbs.

Accepting her faults was never an option for Mom, nor could she recognize her anger at her mother for how she'd been neglected. She could not bear that reality or those feelings, and if she wasn't perfectly good, she must be perfectly bad. If her mom is the saint, and she cannot be like her, and worse yet feel anger toward her, she must be her evil opposite.

I saw this play out in our own family many times over, wherein Mom played the martyred mother and I the disgraceful daughter. Whenever Mom felt aggressive, wanting to either say something mean or even hit me, she provoked me into aggression instead. As she often did with my father, she needed me to act out so that she could jump into the martyr position. She would bait me with pathological reasoning, gaslighting nonsense, frustrating me into a spiral of rage. As a teenager I immediately RSVPed into battle. I'd celebrate in releasing my storm of angst and anger without filters, and she would sigh with secret relief in being attacked. As I hurled verbal grenades she smiled back in haunting satisfaction, as if to say, "See how ugly you are … see what a monster you are to the mother who gave up her life for you." Everything she wanted to say to me but couldn't I was now saying to myself. I felt it all, my anger, her anger, my hate, her hate, my shame, her shame. And I carried it for the both us. Like hot potatoes we threw the demons back and forth but ultimately I felt that I was the one who swallowed them, char and all. Afterward I'd apologize through tears of regret, and she would shoo-shoo me away, dismissively, in saintly absolution.

In Mom's eyes goodness is passivity, an easygoing nature, someone who is nonreactive, and most importantly someone who never, ever rocks the proverbial boat, no matter what. In other words someone exactly like her mother. If there is something direly wrong, hide it, or even better, forget it, "Life is too short, don't get yourself upset." There are no exceptions to the rule, not even domestic violence, molestation, or child abuse. To all sins, Mom is mum. Mum and busy. But sometimes I'd feel compelled to start the conversations regardless.

"You never talked to us about what happened."

"I couldn't help it, I was always so busy."

"For eighteen years?"

"There just was never a good time. I always had something going on. You just don't understand."

"Understand that there wasn't a single moment in eighteen years in which you could have talked to us?"

Mom is silent and angry, clearly with me for bringing "it" up, again.

The "it" in our family is like what happens in a lot of families I work with. The trauma, emotional neglect, and abuse in our family were on the spectrum of dysfunction although, for most of our lives we never viewed it as such. It simply was. But as we become adults with triggers scattered like land mines we are beckoned to their call. Jung believed that the unresolved conflicts of the parents are passed down to the children. Within each of us resides the legacy of unworked issues, and a lost opportunity for wholeness, from what he termed the "unlived life." He stated, "It is hardly ever the open conflict or the manifest difficulty that has such a poisonous effect (on a child's psychological development), but almost always parental problems that have been kept hidden or allowed to become unconscious." Urging parents to do their inner work, he warns that a failure to do so is a moral sin perpetrated upon the children.

Mom's family repressed their thoughts and feelings, burying them in a psychic graveyard. Many of them had OCD as well. Uncle Frank had front door slippers, patio door slippers, pre-shower slippers, post-shower slippers, and bedside slippers; Uncle Fred required two hours of grooming each day. I've been curious over the years as to what dark secrets were interred in the graveyard, feeling there must be at least a skeleton or two. I was certain the measure of their defenses was at least equal to the measure of their wounds and I wondered if Grandma's quiescence was in fact a talent for denial, just as Mom had now mastered.

Mom and her siblings all developed an overcompensating vanity. They wore their pride like armor. But those of us who lived with them saw behind the facade. Beneath the vanity was immense insecurity, guilt, shame, and regret. The contradictions are a tangled web of self-aggrandizing and self-loathing. In one respect Mom knows her beauty all too well. She has studied and assessed herself too many times not to be certain. Yet she hides from the camera like a vampire from sunlight. When she sees herself in photos, she is disgusted with her reflection, consumed with judgment and cringes no matter how perfect the shot. Pictures can't ever live up to what she needs to see, failing to confirm her perfection, as does the photographer fail to capture her beauty.

Whenever my parents had a dinner date, Mom spent hours in the bathroom preparing, throwing her comb at the mirror, in tears. It happened every time without fail. The stress in the house bounced off the walls and sprayed like rubber bullets. There was no hiding from it. Mom would boomerang from bedroom to bathroom and back again, changing her clothes multiple times, cursing and crying and yelling at Dad to "shut up" as he rushed her to make their reservation. When she finally surrendered to her imagined imperfections she would move on to her checking process as Dad waited in the car, leaning on the horn in a rage. Mom would complete her three rounds in the kitchen, checking the appliances from refrigerator to stove to oven ensuring doors were closed and knobs were off and back again, thrice. Finally outside she'd begin door checking our two-family house, from left to right, entry door and screen door right, entry door and screen door left and back again, always three times, pressing urgently on the handles, as Dad screamed though the open window of the Cadillac to "get in the goddamn car already." This was our life with OCD.

CHAPTER 8
La Befana

"Neurotics complain of their illness, but they make the most of it, and when it comes to taking it away from them they will defend it like a lioness her young" —Sigmund Freud

Mom has the diagnostic kind of obsessive-compulsive disorder, not the kind we make jokes about. Most of each day is spent preoccupied by a compulsion to clean and, despite her loathing of the tasks she's obsessed in doing, she cannot stop. As she bends over the toilet scrubbing the already spotless bowl with venomous intent, despair weighs down upon her and suddenly my beautiful mother who typically looks half her age appears haggard. There is a deep-seated wretchedness in her cleansing furor, both ambitious and avoidant, two warring polarities. Like a surgeon resecting a bowel, her mission outweighs the disgust she feels touching contaminated surfaces in pursuit of perfection.

It's a complicated love-hate relationship. She is both troubled and soothed by cleaning. She declares her misery, wearing it like a medal on her apron, devoted and decorated.

She is indentured to the cause, a soldier who must bear the burden for the rest. And simultaneously she fantasizes of a life without witnesses, one in which she can obsess in peace because as excessive as her compulsions are, there are more pushing against the door demanding their turn. She holds back the stampede just short of mutiny, in fear of complete exposure. Surely any argument of sanity would be lost if the brigade were set free.

Mom deeply believed that her compulsions cleansed not just the toilets but her soul. They were a religious virtue, "You know what they say, cleanliness is next to Godliness." This would be her lifelong mantra, as though this bumper sticker cliché legitimized her obsessions, granting them divine approval. God had endorsed her agenda and who or what could ever trump that? The core of Mom's worth, her value in the world, was based solely upon her degree of cleanliness. The commandments are superfluous in comparison.

The religious connection in Mom's cleansing obsessions had me curious over the years. Did her religion, or at least her understanding of religion, make her feel dirty in some way? If not physically, then psychologically or emotionally? Hadn't the church used shame to humble their parishioners, guilt to control their behaviors, punishment to motivate change? Glancing over my caseload, Italian names and OCD diagnoses jumped off the pages. It seemed an unlikely coincidence how many there were. Certainly not a credible study by any means and yet still worthy of exploration I thought. I began to wonder how our ancestors felt living next door to the Vatican's dome of condemnation? How vulnerable were they to shame as a result of the failed pursuit of religious piety? The Catholic concept of original sin runs deep and is contrary to self-acceptance. We take our first breath as sinful beings; it's a tough start. I recall visiting Rome and taking notice of how indifferent Italian business owners were about pleasing their patrons and yet were quite consumed with cleaning around them. I marveled at waiting in a shoe shop for the clerk to finish cleaning the windows before assisting me. The sale seemed an interruption. That "what do you want, can't you see that I'm busy" look was one I knew too well. Even one of their holiday legends is grounded in obsessive cleaning. La Befana was a woman who, because she was too busy cleaning to go to see the Infant Jesus, became a witch with a broom as punishment.

I felt right at home in Italy, not as I expected with the food and culture but rather with the perfectionistic stress. It felt pressured and rushed, a very strange juxtaposition to their otherwise carefree lifestyle of hanging around piazzas chatting, sipping cappuccinos, and waving from scooters—a passive/passionate dichotomy. There were rules for everything mundane and none for things critically important. No cappuccino after noon. No Parmesan cheese on salads. No limoncello before dinner. And no really meant no. No following of the rules? No service Americana! Clip the side view mirror off my car? *Non c'e' problema*. Return a broken appliance? No shot. Make up prices on a daily basis?

You bet. All things of professional protocol or politeness deemed frivolous, but doing things "right" in term of orderliness and aesthetics were of great importance. I suddenly understood Mom from a heritage perspective, this, I thought, is where it originated. They were just like her, scrubbing, sweeping, cleaning, putting things like meals in a working order, this then that. No cappuccino after noon because dairy upsets their digestion, so none for you either. Limoncello is a digestif, so none for you until after your meal. So many rules, restrictions, and rituals, I couldn't help but feel as though they were working hard as hell, just like Mom, to finally wash that original sin away once and for all.

Although Mom considered herself quite religious she admittedly was not a churchgoer. Not even an A&P Catholic as we called them in New York — those who showed up only twice a year, for ashes and palms. Mom did pray a whole lot and in doing so believed she single-handedly ensured our destiny. She asked God to keep each of us safe and fearing she might miss someone or make a mistake in how she prayed she did it repeatedly, over and over again. She believed as her mother did in the *occhio malocchio* or evil eye, however thought the concept of salvation too naive. She viewed life through a superstitious lens, mummifying in the spooky stuff and having an old wive's tale for everything. She feared hell but doubted heaven.

She believed her dreams to be premonitions and some actually were. She predicted events with unsettling accuracy. She believes she saw her mother postmortem in the form of Mother Mary, in a blue glow in the middle of the night. She believes her words have special powers, and fears ending conversations with "goodbye" because God might think she meant it for good. One night I ended our phone conversation with "bye for now" and she excitedly adopted it. The nights before I travel she calls just in case my plane goes down, mostly in fear she'd have a life of regret in not calling, and she can't hang up the phone ever without first saying, "Be safe and well."

She preached to us that life equals suffering and that catastrophic fates hid within dark corners of the universe, just waiting for the unprepared victim, which she was determined none of us would ever be. She armed us for our future, with both eyes on any potential disaster so that even God couldn't catch us off guard. Every crevice of our universe would be safe and clean. And although she did not believe in the afterlife, she assigned a contingency plan just in case…no cremations. God doesn't like those, and besides what if we needed our eyes on the other side?

What could have been had Mom used her faith alternatively, allowed absolution of sin to free her, for faith in an eternal life to comfort her? What could have been had she seen that her healing was inside her the whole time? Like Dorothy's dream, that the answers were in her heart all along, and that she already had everything she needed to be loved? What if instead of flattening her world to hide beneath the radar, she rose above her fears and embraced a more transcendent and affirming dogma?

But Mom didn't take any of the good stuff religion had to offer. She hadn't found community prayer comforting but rather another hurdle she'd have to jump. Everything was a test and a stage on which she would be analyzed and judged, particularly on how she looked. Instead of facing her internal demons she declared church to be a waste of her time. She just couldn't rationalize wasting an hour of her week sitting still and doing nothing. Instead she sent me to church on Sunday mornings, pushing me out the door with a kiss on the cheek and a ten-dollar bill inside an offering envelope, covering another of her moral bases. As she often did, Mom pawned me again, to ease her conflicted soul. So like a good soldier I went to mass at. St. Pius as her proxy, alone and bewildered, sitting in a church pew, perplexed as to why this ancient man waved a smoky orb from the end of a chain at us, clearly trying to choke us all to death. What any of it meant, I had no clue. No one really gave me a reasonable explanation of any of it. Equal parts bored and terrorized, some days I just wanted to skip the whole thing. As I trudged along 147th Ave I swear I heard that ten-dollar bill calling me, a divine intervention, because I could actually see Hamilton's eye wink at me through the window slit of that blue envelope and instead of entering the sacred house of the Lord, I detoured south toward town to spend God's money on pizza and an egg cream, and one very large goody bag filled with colorful jawbreakers. Mom's conscience would rest but mine would have to do some work at a later date. In the meantime I avoided the shadow of guilt that forever stalked behind me.

But it all catches up with us. Catholic blood flows through my veins and plaques of shame are constantly breaking off, clogging up the psychological pipelines. Every mishap feels gargantuan, every bit of self-care like greedy self-indulgence. Confessional booth disclosures were like pouring gasoline on self-condemnation, and alchemizing childhood innocence into moral leprosy. Catholics are gaslighted into believing in our inherent badness, and between Dad's Sicilian upbringing and Mom's OCD the shame was reinforced tenfold. Mistakes were magnified everywhere I went.

With Dad, who had a sensory issue, every noise and light was glaringly agitating to him. A closet door that clicked, a heavy footstep above him, clanking dishes, all made him crazed. He'd scream at us as though mundane actions were mortal sins. With Mom, it was every thing I touched that was made to feel spoiled. I wasn't allowed to take a shower on the main floor like everyone else but rather in the finished basement because I left too much water behind. It was a mystery to me how they all kept the spray inside the shower curtain and felt it was pretty infuriating that I couldn't. I hated showering down there, juggling my clothes, blow dryer, and brushes down into the freezing cold and I was angry I couldn't measure up in even cleansing myself. In surrender I'd just add it to the long list of ineptitudes.

But despite the chronicity of these micro-rejections I never fully succumbed to their conditioning, I didn't buy into their versions of who I was and never consciously thought them right. I knew at times it was their own issues causing problems and not mine. But I didn't think them entirely wrong either. I felt in my body that I was fundamentally bad in some way, that they knew me in a way I didn't know myself, and I was terrified of ever meeting that version of myself. That's the dialectical at work. Two polarities coexisting, neither one completely right or wrong, but rather both working simultaneously. When we see patients who have traumatic backgrounds we have to work with what they *know* to be true as well as what they *feel* to be true as the two are often conflicting. Often they will say, "I know I am worthy but I feel like I am garbage." For me, I *knew* I was the sane one in the family but I *felt* like I was the one who was crazy. I had to work for years to break out of those mind washing cognitions, challenging them while also processing the underlying emotions. When it comes to psychological trauma changing our thinking is complicated. Proving that two plus two equals four and not five gets stored in memory simply, but when emotional pain is associated with the information, adaptive reasoning gets sidelined. The scar tissue around the stored memory makes it inaccessible to logic and fact. We have to break through that barrier by processing the original emotions, neurologically opening the path to reprocessing. In this way what we know and how we feel gets aligned. For example, a patient needed to process feelings of abandonment and rejection from when her mother left her alone as a child to go partying with strange men. She knew she didn't deserve to be neglected as a child, yet her loathing for that frightened child remained. Instead of being angry at her parent, her only source of survival, she hated herself. All the reasoning in the world couldn't change her feelings about it. However, when we focused on dropping into the emotions of the experience and allowing herself to feel the pain of the child, we were able to introduce new information and in essence speak to the child in a way the child could understand. The neurological pathways were open to new learning and she was able to reprocess the memory adaptively. After several sessions the patient began feeling empathy and love for the child and thus able to feel her innocence versus her shame. Eventually she was able to direct her anger to the source— her mother, and free herself from all the repressed rage she had internalized and carried for so many years.

CHAPTER 9
Italian Sacrilege

"The people who give you their food give you their heart,"
—Cesar Chavez

Italians and Sunday dinners are a thing. No self-respecting Italian family bypasses the tradition. Mom starts the sauce in the morning and by 5 p.m. it has grown rich in meat renderings and cooked to perfection. The house is filled with the pleasantly pungent aroma of simmering gravy. Not sauce, but gravy!

Dinners are spent around long tables with extended family for several courses and as many hours. First is the antipasto of meats and cheeses, then the main course of pasta, then meat, then salad, then dessert with espresso and Sambuca for the adults. These dinners are the essence and expression of family love, in the verb. It's what we do.

For Mom, Sunday dinners were hell. She abhorred every part of it, except for the compliments on her lasagna. Those she ate up eagerly. She begrudged the work, hated cooking, resented the clean up, and complained no one helped her although we all pitched in. There wasn't family gathering around the kitchen while she cooked, with small talk and sipped wine. There wasn't laughter or celebration or any signs of happiness in being together. She cooked alone because we got in her way and did it wrong, so we stayed clear. It was obligatory work, or worse, some kind of punishment for her to cook for her family. If she put love in the food she prepared I couldn't taste it. What I did detect was a deep resentment stirring.

During dinner Dad oohed and aahed, Aunt Julie groaned in delight, and we all showed our gratitude for a delicious meal. It was our job to make Mom feel appreciated and we showed up with our best flattery. After dinner, the men sat at the table cracking walnuts and sipping more Sambuca as the women got up to clean the dishes. We worked until it was all cleared away and then hustled off to watch TV, lying on the floor on our full bellies. But Mom wouldn't join us, she stayed in the kitchen until 10 p.m. continuing to clean. We had no idea what was left but she cleaned and cleaned until she was too tired to do anymore. One night we spied on her to see just what she was doing. My sister and I watched as she took a sponge across a clean counter, then back to the clean table and back to the sink again where she touched either side of the faucet three times before the next rotation. When she finally collapsed on the recliner she complained that we never help her and she never gets a break like the rest of us. I felt guilty, but I didn't know what it was I was guilty for.

After my sister and brother left home Mom decided she wasn't going to cook anymore. She had done her time and since we didn't appreciate her why should she bother. My father shrugged his shoulders and I suspect it was hardly a surrender as much as it was relief. Mom's cooking had dwindled down to dinners of overcooked meat and vegetables turned upside out of a can. No more Sunday dinners as my aunts rarely visited anymore. On Dad's middle-income salary we ate out four nights a week after Mom's declaration and by the time Dad retired he had bupkis in the bank.

When I met my partner Lisa, and began spending Sunday dinners with her family, I felt like I was on the set of Moonstruck. I had no idea that kind of thing was for real. There was cooking with actual merriment, lively chatter and laughter, playfulness and love, lots and lots of love. I was happy and grateful and sad all at once.

CHAPTER 10
And the Wheels Go Round and Round

"The more perfect a person is on the outside, the more demons they have on the inside." —Sigmund Freud

For Mom, living with OCD was like running on multiple hamster wheels, none of them ever leading anywhere but to the next. Completing one compulsion only meant she was now free for another, and there is always another. There are two goals, to complete this task, ritual, or compulsion, and to have another in queue. Not having something else to do means she could be still and that is her kryptonite. The result of a study published in Science Magazine in 2014 found that when participants were given a choice between sitting in a room doing nothing at all or electing to administer electric shocks on themselves, two-thirds of the men and a quarter of the women elected to shock themselves. It's hard for any healthy person to sit alone with their feelings and thoughts, but for someone with OCD it is often unbearable. When a thought arises we all feel compelled to get up and do the thing that enters our mind, but for those with OCD it is absolutely intolerable not to engage. When that pile of books needs to be squared off, it must be done now.

Sitting still with obsessive thoughts creates a discomfort even those without OCD can appreciate but it also is a functioning dysfunction. It is the psyches' way of attempting to relieve the pressure from real life worries that people may feel powerless to rectify. Sterilizing one's hands is controllable, and therefore comforting. Although the obsessive thought is intrusive, demanding, and all consuming, it is unconsciously (subconsciously?) welcomed as it functions to offset greater stress. Some analysts theorize that OCD is the result of a double-bind, a catch-22 of sorts where no good option exists. Should I leave my alcoholic partner or stay for the sake of the family? Should I confront my husband's anger at the risk of having it turned on me or let the children (who I believe are resilient) absorb it? Should I...? When the toss-up gets locked within analysis paralysis the symptoms of OCD generally will intensify.

Sometimes the conscious mind gets pulled into past regrets, guilt, shame, and the like as it does for all of us. But for the OCD sufferer those thoughts are highly ignitable, vulnerable to perfectionistic thinking, an inability to accept fault, and immense shame. Rather than work with those thoughts and feelings they often will get busy again in avoidance. While some are willing to work hard in breaking this merry-go-round process by confronting the sources of their pain, Mom is not. She's not keen on reflection and introspection. With no irony or self-awareness her frequent words of advice are "Just don't think about bad things, think good thoughts." That's the OCD function of repress and deny in a nutshell. I'm not disputing the benefits of positive thinking, but when your house is on fire, telling yourself otherwise is just a poor strategy.

What lurks in Mom's suppressed mind is anyone's guess, and I doubt if Mom even has any idea what she is running away from. I suspect her secrets are a mixture of innocuous and horrific. I have seen how the benign alchemizes into full-blown malignancy in a maddening use of "logic." If two things occur together in Mom's world they are not only related but causative.

The night before my grandmother died Mom reluctantly accepted an invitation to play Mahjong. Her mother was never especially well and this night was like any other. There wasn't any type of imminent threat, nothing that she ignored in leaving. So she went out. She rarely enjoyed socializing but her friends needed a fourth player so she went. The next day, Grandma had an aortic aneurysm and died in my mother's arms on the bathroom floor. Despite being there at the moment of my grandmother's last breath, holding her in her arms no less, Mom has carried lifelong guilt for not spending their last night together. That is perhaps not completely out of the realm of normalcy when it comes to grief especially, but deeper in my mother's mind she abandoned her mother and that is why she died. In her reasoning and her all-encompassing superego powers, she alone is responsible for this tragic event. It's always the child's fault. Everything that happens in the child's world is caused by the child and Mom is stuck in this egocentric stage. It's her default mode. The guilt she feels about her mother's death has endured without diminishment for nearly sixty years and her nightmare is that it someday repeats itself. Now she hovers over her 93-year-old sister, unable to leave her side and risk not being there in her final hours. She has an aversion to Mahjong, as though the white tiles are cursed. Sometimes she blames her friends for convincing her to play, other times she blames the game itself, but always she winds up angry, ashamed of herself for abandoning her mother believing that her selfishness was what finally killed her.

The endless looping in Mom's brain ensnarls her in this nonsensical cycle without resolution. Sometimes she is influenced by our reasoning but within minutes she's right back in it again. "Mom, Grandma was sick for years, and you were there when she died. You have to know it wasn't your fault." As I say the words Mom silently nods her head, tilting to one side offering me a ray of hope, "Maybe you're right. I hope you're right."

I get sucked into the cycle like a reflex, I can't resist the need to fix her thinking, hoping that maybe this one time I can finally help her to see what is real, help diminish her anxiety or guilt; but the highs of helping are always followed by the lows of relapses. When I debate her logic she reacts as though I am either ignorant or mocking when in reality I am neither, but rather attempting to reason with the unreasonable. I am persistent in wasting my energy. I do this perhaps in part because of the past. In Mom's denial of her

OCD she blamed us for her hardships. Because we existed she had work to do. As children we didn't understand that we were not responsible for our mother's unhappiness, nor were we her slaveholders as she called us. There was only one real master in the house and that was the disorder. Three letters that held all the power in the world and demanded her perpetual busyness and orderliness and misery. OCD, an illness that infects like a virus. It has been my personal nemesis and a cruel interloper in my relationship with Mom. When it shows its face, seeking to divide me from her, my instinct is to pounce, first with reason, then with anger.

Her compulsions get deposited in my in my lap like unfinished puzzles to solve. Last week she interrupted me at work because she needed the landscaper over to her house right away. She communicates this to me like a crisis, "Why does it have to be today?" I ask, knowing full well she is in the midst of some yet to be identified obsession. Much like the discussion about where to eat, we can't ever get to it directly, we have to first go through the protocol of my chasing her around until she finally gets to the real issue. Getting increasingly irritated, I play the game until finally she says, "Well, the housecleaner is coming this afternoon" (yes, a compulsive cleaner needs a housecleaner too).

"And?" I prompt her for the full confession.

"And I want the landscapers to make their mess with their blowers before she comes. Then I can have her clean the patio furniture and put the covers on," she says.

Okay so that makes sense, I think, hardly an emergency

but she should have the furniture cleaned before putting the covers on. But the bigger question remains why do the landscaper and the housecleaner have to do this on the same day? Why can't the housecleaner clean the chairs any time after the landscaper comes? "Well," she says, "this way the chairs and the covers will be clean together."

"Ok," I say, "but tomorrow the covers will be dusty because we do live in the desert."

"Yes, but at least they will both be clean today."

I made the mistake of getting patio furniture for her when she said she'd love to sit outside. Wow, I thought, that would be an amazing shift away from her depressing housebound existence. So I excitedly went shopping and bought a cute little bistro set for her and her sister to enjoy. The prospect of her sitting outside sipping her morning cappuccino delighted me more than it would have any sane person. I still go to the empty well carrying my buckets despite constantly reminding my patients not to do the same. But there I am climbing uphill with a pole across my shoulders, thirsty and thrilled.

It's been three years now and she hasn't sat on the chairs yet. However, they were then added to her list of burdens since they need to be cleaned and in the Arizona heat that can be a quite unpleasant task. This is where the covers came into play. When she asked that I buy them to keep the dust off I knew that was the end of the outdoor bistro fantasy permanently. This week she upped the game and asked me to get her a patio umbrella to keep the covers clean. She didn't say it that way, but baited me with another round of hope, as though she wanted to enjoy the patio in the sun, not to keep the covers, that were keeping the chairs, clean. But I wasn't going to be fooled again.

Six months after my father passed away Mom moved to Arizona so that I could help take care of her. Packing up her house in Florida was quite the experience, as was setting her up here. For months she talked about needing a new coffee table and area rug for the living room. I shopped with her in the stores and online and nothing was right. After my patience ran out she said that she couldn't buy an area rug without first knowing the color of the table. "Ok," I said, "then let's focus on the table first" and showed her over twenty different ones. None would work she said. Why? Because she didn't know which would go with the area rug that she still hadn't picked out. "Let me get this straight" I barked, "you can't get the table before the rug, or the rug before the table?" to which she looked at me blankly. These catch-22 scenarios are relentless and still manage to amaze me. While it's hard to imagine what it feels like to have a brain that works this way, it truly tests ones sanity. Now when she asks me a trapping question like "Do you think I need a colonoscopy?" (despite the doctor telling her she should not at her age), I answer "That's between you and your OCD." She sees it as disrespectful, I see it as self-preservation.

Everything has rules and order without exceptions. While my father was in rehab, post-surgery for an aggressive and ultimately fatal glioblastoma, the nurse asked us to bring him sneakers because he was slipping on the floors in his grippy socks and had almost fallen that morning. I reminded my mother to bring them repeatedly but she claimed to have forgotten each time. Finally I sat her down and said, "What is it now, what craziness is keeping you from bringing Dad his sneakers?" Admittedly not my finest moment, confirmed by the nasty look she shot my way, as she retorted "They're dirty!" "They're dirty," I echoed. "You're not bringing them because they're dirty?" As we yell back and forth I follow her to the closet where she bends over picking up the sneakers and holding them up like a prosecutor revealing the murder weapon and says, "Look at the soles," confident in her case. "The soles!" the words come out of my mouth in a shrill, all semblance of self-control completely lost. My father's life was ending, all of us were thick in anticipated grief and instead of processing the experience together, comforting and supporting each other, we were fighting about the bottoms of Dad's shoes. "I swear to God Mom, we are bringing them to him tomorrow," I said grinding my teeth in attempted restraint.

The next day Mom angrily surrenders, wraps Dad's sneakers in three plastic grocery bags and brings them to the hospital. When I arrived later that day a nurse stops me to say Dad really needs his sneakers. I let her know that Mom had brought them earlier in the day and she looked at me as if to say, "Okay but I don't think so." Marching into his room, my rage ready to ignite, I search through his things and there they were, triple wrapped and hidden in the back of his closet behind his laundry bag. No one would find them and yet Mom could feel she complied, once again she would lose the battle but win the war. It broke my heart to see Dad so glaringly neglected and when I should have been preparing myself for his inevitable passing I spent much of that time in a constant state of fury.

My parents were married for sixty-two years. Mom was twenty-one when they married, Dad twenty-two. While theirs was not a marriage you want modeled for your children, they loved each other. My mother's love for him was like Golde's for Tevye, for twenty-five years she washed his clothes, cooked his meals, cleaned his house, gave him children…if that's not love, what is? My father on the other hand adored my mother like a schoolboy crush up until his very last breath. Despite his having severe anger issues and their having a brutal beginning to their marriage they remained together for more than half a century. I would oscillate as a child between wanting her to leave him and him to leave her. They were that tied in dysfunction. In many respects they were perfect for each other and in many more they were each other's worst nightmare. But their generation was never quick to divorce and I don't think Mom would have survived on her own. When my partner and I got married she thanked her parents for teaching her how to have a loving relationship. I thanked mine for teaching me perseverance. We laughed when we wrote it, but it was a sober truth.

Dad and I talked a lot in those final weeks, even though he'd had a stroke and was delusional at times. We had not gotten along for the past four decades but after his brain was rewired by a stroke, he was an entirely different man. He became undefended with nothing to prove. His once narcissistic and grandiose persona vanished and a kind, gentle, loving man emerged. For two months he was the father I had always longed for. If his delusions weren't so tragically sad, they would have been entertaining. My sister brought him a small plastic statuette of Padre Pio, the Franciscan monk, that sat propped up in a windowed box to bring him healing power (we were desperate at the time), and we found it one day out of the box and under his bed. We asked him what happened and he said it was hard as a rock. He thought it was a chocolate Easter treat. My sister and I laughed in that bittersweet moment fully realizing how gone his brain had become. But Mom would laugh joyfully as though at a party, his delusions the opening act, saying, "Your father is so funny all of a sudden. I never knew he had such a sense of humor." She wouldn't believe that he had become delusional as a result of the stroke and in fact thought his humor a positive sign. She didn't believe he would actually die, this despite the doctors' blunt diagnosis and Dad's subsequent admittance to hospice.

In one of Dad's hallucinations he envisioned my mother having a sword hanging on her back and asked me in a hoarse whisper why she wanted to hurt him. His face was heartbreakingly sad, like a little boy, hurt and confused. I assured him Mom wasn't going to use that sword but I couldn't help but sense the irony of his vision. She had samurai-ed his heart over the years. We'd found poems he'd written before he had the stroke, prose of defeat and surrender. She would never love him the way he needed, and he dwelled lower on the OCD ladder than any of us. I asked him in those final days if he still loved my mother and his eyes shot at me so hard it rattled me, nodding his head emphatically, as though I were insane to ask. The truth was I almost hoped he didn't. I was that angry.

It was a relief that his condition precluded him from seeing my mother's neglect of him in the hospital. It would not have surprised him but a respite from awareness was a kind of blessing. Ignorance was bliss in the end. That even his impending death would fail to be an exception to her compulsions was the coldest of realities and I was grateful he could be spared this one time. But for the rest of us, we were captive witnesses to the magnitude of Mom's dysfunction as she showed up each day, physically sitting beside him but in a completely mindless state. She wouldn't think to bring him food despite our stopping on the way for our own, she didn't notice the gash on the side of his head from sleeping with his glasses on, she ignored the doctors orders on how to safely feed him, laughing when I corrected her. Yes, grief and shock were evident, but again, it would not have mattered if Dad were in for a tonsillectomy, she would have had the same response.

On the surface of it, Mom can seem heartless and cruel, even sadistic. It takes a miraculous moment of presence to stop and say to myself "This is not who your mother is, it's what she has that makes her act this way." But more times than not that presence is unreachable and the only time I can be objective is when I have distance enough to think clearly.

Sadly, the sicker Dad got the sicker Mom got as well. By the time of his death, she had become entirely nonsensical to the point of questioning if he was actually dead in the casket. She declined to come with my siblings and me to the service planning, and we did our best trying to guess what she would want, choosing the casket and urn for cremation (Dad wanted cremation and Mom tried to override it but this battle she lost). She insisted on a closed casket service so we elected not to have his body embalmed. The funeral director advised against any viewing and we said we understood. None of us elected to see Dad in this state. When we got home Mom asked my sister and me to view Dad's body for her. "Why?" we asked. "Just please do it for me, okay, I can't rest until you do." We told her no, because the body hadn't been prepared and it had been a few days since he had died. In tears she pleaded harder, "Please, I have to know he is really dead. I have to be sure. Maybe he's not. Maybe they just think he's dead." This insanity, that he could be alive in a mortuary with no one's knowledge for days, coupled with her unwillingness to experience the grief and pain of proving or disproving it herself, multiplied by her demand that we do so in her stead, very willing to put her children through that pain and grief, was a crushing offense and I felt assaulted and prostituted by her OCD, and if I can tell the whole truth, by her. The casual observer would correctly see an elderly, fragile, grieving widow who'd just lost her husband of 63sixty-three years being dismissed by her three competent adult children in her greatest moment of vulnerability and fear. If I could have summoned a genie I would have wished for the sensitivity she needed, however having spent my life in the crucible of her OCD I not only did not have the empathy, patience or tolerance the situation seemed to require, I could not even summon a superficial version of it. And I felt like shit. The slim emotional reed I held on to was that my brother and sister similarly refused.

Mom couldn't see our grief. Our father hadn't passed away but only her husband. She didn't ask how we were doing, or what we were feeling, it had never occurred to her. Once again, we couldn't process as a family; another missed opportunity for strengthening our relationships. We experienced Dad's illness as though it was happening to us separately and I felt detached from her pain, and perhaps my own as well.

On the day of the service, we helped Mom get seated in the viewing room. She was distraught but holding it together for the moment, greeting people and accepting condolences. As family and friends took their seats, she went over to the casket, kneeling down to pray. I stood by her partly for support but also because I anticipated a need for damage control. I can usually sense the beginnings of an episode, like an aura before a migraine. She had her hand on top of the casket and began talking to Dad, through the cherrywood, asking if he was in there. Louder and louder she began yelling, "Vinny, are you in there? Vinny!" I tried to quiet her, this grief stricken eighty-four-year-old woman, at first gently, but as her hysterics intensified, my need for control escalated, and I told her "Stop!" through gritted teeth, pulling her back to her seat. I felt humiliated and like an insensitive brute at my own need for order.

I have seen the shock of loss do strange things to people and I understand the immensity of its impact on those left behind and yet Mom's display that day was not an anomaly, but a continuity of her usual madness. She had seen for herself that he was gone, been there minutes after Dad was pronounced dead, even sat with him for over an hour at his bedside, and still the reality hadn't set in.

Mom has a pattern of these kinds of histrionic events. Often they are a result of her inability to deal with the feelings or stress of the situation. Whenever she gets bad news she collapses, reminiscent of the vapors that gave women a bad name a hundred years ago—that is, hysterical. But there are also less theatrical collapses that are staged manipulations, with a clear agenda. If she feels trapped in an argument she will break out one of these acts in which she throws herself to the floor, feigning a death wish, "I'll just die then, just kill me." Her face will droop and her eyes roll, as though life has suddenly drained from her body and life's cruel reality is simply too much to stand, literally. If I call her out on something that I find hurtful she will similarly surrender to a wish for death. I cannot hide my reaction, or lack thereof, as my face exposes every bit of the coldness I feel. I am utterly without feeling, like a sudden power outage everything goes dark inside me. The unavailability of my emotions only convinces her, or anyone who might be witnessing the show, that I am certainly a sociopath, "How can you stand there looking like you don't care?" she asks in astonishment. She tells herself that I am a monster, which can be the only explanation for my lack of compassion. Perhaps the shutting down of my heart is cruel, as she says; however, it doesn't happen by will. It's organic. I feel nothing, utter numbness. I can attempt to defend myself explaining that it is the direct result of being manipulated for so many years and that yielding to these "acts" would be my demise. Or I can argue that in giving in to her hysterics I enable the continuance of this behavior, rewarding it. But in the final accounting I seemingly land on the wrong side of history, and am subsequently left questioning my very humanity.

It wasn't until people outside of my family began to witness these scenes and reassure me that I wasn't the villain I had been made to be, that I began to question myself for the better. The possibility that I had been gaslighted for so many years and was no longer able to discern what was real from what was not was ground breaking and ground shaking. To question everything I had been taught, that had been chiseled into my psyche, shattered my foundation; and despite it having been a faulty one, it was still the solid form beneath my feet versus the free fall of nothingness. What is truth after all, if not my own experience? If I couldn't trust my own experience then what? My reasoning failed to consider that my interpretations of my experiences were tweaked and tainted by my parents, by my environment. I resisted believing their condemnations of me, yet I grew to feel them. Like little insidious seeds planted in my psyche, they gave life to insecurity, confusion, self-doubts.

I must have known intuitively that I needed strong advocates as friends and partners. People who would support me with honest feedback and who were unafraid to call it as they saw it. I depended on their eyes and ears because mine were not trustworthy. And when I let them in to the world of mirrors they helped me to see what was real. Only then did I felt safe enough to loosen my grip on my own faulty data, to question the seeds that had sprouted so much self-doubt. My perspective started to shift ever so slightly and my memories began to thicken like a plot, with layers of new clues. It then grew possible to consider that just maybe my family had a role in the dysfunction and that I alone was not the problem. My ability to dissociate from my experiences perhaps meant that I had developed a coping mechanism without which I may have lost my own sanity. Just maybe I was not the compassionless animal I was made to feel and that a blowout of my breaker was an ingenious defense of my psyche deserving of gratitude, not shame.

CHAPTER 11
Mired in Stone

"He wanted to live in a house built on delusion, would rather
believe in a million lies than face one truth."
—Marie Lu, *The Rose Society*

One challenging characteristic of OCD is the inflexibility of rigid thought. Completely immune to logic and reason it has the power to neutralize and disregards facts. Most people with OCD do realize that their thinking is irrational but are unable to alter their reactions nonetheless. Reality is simply irrelevant.

But Mom buys into her compulsive thoughts completely. Other people are the problem, the ones with faulty reasoning. Anyone who would not scrub like a surgeon after using the bathroom is clearly ignorant. Once Mom makes a connection, no matter the reality, it is permanent and no amount of fact, logic, or persuasion will alter that connection. She believes she has private access to the real facts, the secret ones hidden from the rest of us. We are unawakened beings.

For better or worse, I have inherited from her an ability for quick associations and a memory that keeps them accessible. Fortunately, it is a great benefit in my work. I imagine it would be an unfortunate talent otherwise, as I am tireless in my own self-analysis and preoccupations. Unfortunately for Mom her OCD runs crappy analyses and her quick connections yield constrictive versus expansive thinking. Her faulty assumptions are immediately concretized and she becomes obsessed with validating inaccuracies. She hears what she needs for confirmation and dismisses anything that refutes it.

Mom uses associations to comfort her anxiety and feelings of powerlessness and she seeks patterns as a way of making sense out of a senseless world. Three people she knew in Florida died in a relatively short period of time, three very old people, who all came from somewhere in the state of Pennsylvania. People she knew were dying left and right as they do in retirement communities, ambulances were a daily sighting. But she became fixated about these three deaths for weeks, bringing it up in conversation repeatedly, "What could the connection be?" she'd ask, certain there must be one. "I don't know what's happening, why are all these people from Pennsylvania dying all of a sudden?" she'd anxiously lament.

Putting everything in categories helps Mom avoid inevitable realities like death. If she could identify the connection she could, in her mind, control it. Oh, they died because people from Pennsylvania are big meat eaters and meat blocks your arteries. I don't eat much meat, ergo

I won't die. She perseverated for months about how and why Dad could possibly have gotten brain cancer when he was so smart, "I don't understand, your father was always using his brain, reading and doing puzzles, he was always thinking, how could his brain get cancer like that, I just don't understand." She once feared she had caught AIDS because her osteoporosis injections were in the same refrigerator as someone's HIV medication. She began convincing herself she was tired and weak and that she must have at least contracted hepatitis B, because in her mind if you don't get AIDS from exposure you can at least get something like the hepatitis virus. She insisted the doctor do a blood test despite his bafflement and reluctance. When we were children she warned us not to smoke, especially as girls, because it would make hair grow on our breasts. How, you ask? Well, smoking is a man's thing, something women don't do, and men have hair on their chests so…

I spent a lot of energy challenging her, attempting to reason with her beliefs. Hearing my own logic out loud gave me some semblance of sanity. But she'd look at me as vacant as a droid and I knew my attempts were absolutely futile. Once in a great while she might throw me a bone and feign agreement, "Oh I see what you're saying. Three people from Pennsylvania who died are just a small and random percentage. Maybe you're right." But the next day she'd be back there again. We couldn't agree on a reality and nothing ever overlapped in terms of our thoughts and ideas. She was unrelatable to me and I to her.

Mom sees all connections as causal relationships, believing that A is not just correlated to B, but also causes B. She was diagnosed with anemia at eighty-five years old after she had taken a fall and was badly bruised. Surprisingly she did not break any bones but she was laid up for several weeks with severe pain. Because the diagnosis and the fall occurred within a short period of time Mom fused the two things in her mind and believed that the fall caused the anemia. It has been three years since the fall and she is still anemic, and yet she continues to blame the fall. After attempting to debate the merits of her logic I ask with sarcasm, "You have been bleeding internally for three years?" to which she replied with a shrug, "It could happen,". I then spend the better part of an hour wasted in further attempts at reason, "But Mom, after Dad died you were really depressed and wouldn't eat and still have not been eating right. When is the last time you ate meat? You only have it once every month or two. Malnutrition and vitamin B deficiency are the most common causes of anemia, especially at your age. Don't you think that makes more sense?" This all of course shouting till my throat hurts so that she can hear me despite being 90 percent deaf. She doesn't need hearing aids, we need stronger vocal cords, she doesn't say that but you know she thinks it. I am not a shouter and it literally stresses me to communicate with her and its really hard to convey my feelings when everything comes across breaking the sound barrier. When I hear myself I detect a mean tone, although I'm not intending one, because its hard to shout gently. I've begun avoiding long conversations, but this one seemed to compel me despite a tiring day. I'm yelling the last line and she looks at me exhausted even though it's me doing all the heavy lifting and says, "Well I guess I can think about it." Then, ending with a patronizing pat on my hand, she adds "My daughter the doctor," fully aware that I am not that kind of doctor. When I go home I drop onto the bed in a full body dive, feeling just a tiny bit more useless than the day before. The effect on me is cumulative, and each morning I attempt to recalibrate, turning to my personal protocol in sanity maintenance; yoga, meditation, exercise. I took on this role to care for Mom in her last years. I can't say why I made that call only that I knew as the invitation left my lips that it was my destiny making the decision. I was her first caretaker after her mother died, and now I'd be her last. Some part of me needed to come to the surface to show its face and be worked through. Maybe Mom and I needed to do something together to resolve the old conflicts and wounds. I didn't know, I just knew to surrender to it. Tomorrow will bring more trials and I tell myself that I'm learning something living through this, perhaps it's patience, perhaps compassion. I trust my journey so I try to meet it each day with a renewed openness, view my problems as challenges, not enemies. I will flounder and fail, but I am also evolving as the layers are peeled back one-by-one, exposing themselves at times mercilessly. Slowly I start to see my need to help her and save her from herself as my own issue, my own need for control. My analyst never tires of reminding me of this. Attempting to right Mom's ship is not only futile but a distraction from what is real. It is a disembodiment of present experience. I resist my pain, sadness, grief, and longing by brutally fighting against what is, rather than yielding with love and compassion. Our human nature tells us this is the better choice, don't allow vulnerability, a soft heart is death; fight, fight, fight. As if a difficult emotion will devour us, which sometimes it does, and yet we get up the next day and the next. So what are we really so afraid of? Our feelings don't really kill us, we just treat them like they will. When I coach myself to sit and be with the emotion it's never as bad as I expect but what is, is the resisting. That is a chronic and exhausting kind of suffering. The feelings come and go, but the fighting is endless. When I can, in the rare moment, realize this as it's happening I can let go of fixing Mom and feel love and compassion in place of anger and blame. Stop righting her ship, I remind myself, and right my own when sailing rough waters.

The inability to have a real relationship with Mom is of course the most painful consequence of her disorder. When she becomes fixated upon her ideas she pushes you out like an unwelcome guest, as if to say, "You're not wanted here, nor are your facts." It's her own fake news defense and, like it does in politics, it leads to a tenuous grip on one's sanity and sense of hope. It feels like perpetual defeat and eventually you just stop reading the headlines. But then everyone in your orbit tells you about them anyway, "Did you hear the news today?" "No," and like the rest of the country I don't want to know at this point. But despite your saying no, you get sucked in again. My sister is my headline news updater. Despite living 2000 miles away she speaks to Mom daily. More often than not she knows more about what's going on with Mom than I do and Mom lives four blocks from me. She calls when she gets home from a night out to let Mom know she got home okay. If she drives from New York to New Jersey she calls Mom to let her know she is safe. She is sixty years old and has not been able to cut the cord to Mom's anxiety. On the rare occasion that she doesn't remember to call, Mom will panic, call me and spill out in alarm, "Have you heard from Donna? Where could she be now? Why hasn't she called?". They have set up a system that allows no margin for error.

When I take a needed break and disengage from Mom's compulsions, ignoring her house crises or illness fantasies I have my sister to re-engage me. She will call asking about doctor's visits and test results and she'll even call the doctors directly to assist in diagnosing and treating Mom. Then she and Mom build on each other's anxiety until both are convinced Mom is most certainly dying. I am excluded from their process because of my refusal to engage and they treat my frustration and annoyance as the problem. My sister will remind me that Mom is afraid to tell me things as though my reaction is inappropriate. As Dad would say, I am mercurial.

But if one's blood pressure rises due to a gun to one's head I'm thinking the spike is not really the problem.

They say even a broken clock is right twice a day and the one time my sister's hypochondria proved right, it wound up being the ultimate hole-in-one. At eighty-four years old my father was beginning to be more and more forgetful, more often losing his sense of direction, quieter, and even under-reacting to slights. Always fearful of the worst-case scenario, my sister became worried that my father's symptoms were indicative of brain cancer and implored his doctors to run tests. They were reluctant for weeks but eventually agreed to do a scan, likely to fend off my sister who can be tireless in her pursuit of reassurance. During this waiting period, she and Mom continually drilled me with worry, causing me to armor up. I raised my shield, defending myself against anxiety contagion and deduced that their fear was just more nonsense. When my sister asked what I thought was wrong with Dad I said it sounded a lot like depression, which would be reasonable given his life at the time. He had begun limiting his contact with everyone, staying in his room either on his iPad or watching TV, coming out only to do food shopping and taking Mom and her sister to dinner like the chauffeur he was. He knew he was an object of use for them, only as good as his ability to keep them happy. My conjectures, however, wound up being an epic misstep. While he may have been depressed, the scan showed a fatally aggressive cancer that would take his life in less than two months. The move from caregiver to infirm was startlingly quick. As for dismissing any cries of wolf in the future, I have lost some bit of confidence in my shield of reason.

Each member of our family has a different form of OCD as well as a different way of coping with Mom's. Siblings rarely use the same defense mechanism, as if there is only one of each to go around. Where my sister is enmeshed, my brother is detached. He closes out the stress chanting his Mind Over Matter anthem. He can remove himself from conflict without leaving the room. Like, Mom he has OCD but rejects the diagnosis saying, "I can control my compulsions, I just choose not to." He has a number of rules about how he eats his Cheerios, for example. He is a rigid thinker, cannot live outside of his lines, and where Dad ruled us with an iron fist, my brother clothes his in the velvet glove. His preferences become his family's through indoctrination and as they accept these preferences any variance is met with his cold rejection; the withdrawal of his approval is powerful, as Mom's was for us. No makeup, no nail polish, no alcohol, no religion, no new music and yet he sees himself as open-minded, flexible, and non-judgmental. He will often say they (his family) can do what they want but denies the influence of his disapproval. He believes himself to be an advocate to the underdog, yet fails to see how he disempowers those he loves most.

My sister and my mother are of the same cloth. They process the world similarly and are fused. They use external stress as a way of channeling their internal conflicts and will ruminate in endless circles of thought. There is little daylight between them, their Venn diagram greatly eclipsed. Both have more severe OCD symptoms albeit different sets. Like Attention Deficit Disorder there are many subtypes. Both of them have hypochondria and obsess about subtle changes in their bodies as well as the health of loved ones. Both need constant assurance of safety but where Mom is risk-phobic my sister is rather a daredevil. It's as though her reality is backward and the real threats don't register while imagined ones terrorize her. She has very different obsessions and compulsions than Mom. The difference between obsessions and compulsions are that the former are thought-related and the latter behavior-related.

Obsessions are unwanted, intrusive thoughts, images, or urges that trigger intensely distressing feelings. Compulsions are behaviors one engages in, in an attempt to stop the obsessions and/or decrease the distress. My sister has a history of picking her face, at imagined imperfections, to the point of scarring. It causes her horrible distress, yet she is unable to stop. Theoretically the compulsion helps the psyche to manage her repressed trauma. She also doesn't feel compelled to clean like Mom, and in fact lacks motivation in doing so, but rather addictively scrolls on her technology like a foam roller for the brain.

I clearly share the diagnosis with the rest of my family. Along with my mother and sister, I began taking Zoloft, an antidepressant that effectively treats OCD. I felt it was needed when I got into a serious relationship and realized that living with me could be an unpleasant endeavor. I felt it important to protect my loved one more than I felt a need to treat my symptoms. They were agitating and uncomfortable but they didn't impair my quality of life or so I thought. But as I began to realize the things that comforted my obsessions were things that troubled my partner I knew I needed to do something. When friends with children came over I couldn't relax and enjoy the company, but rather fixated on every move the child made with his Rocket Pop in hand. Even sitting at the kitchen table made me horribly anxious, as though a sticky table would be my actual demise. My discomfort was obvious to others and like my mother I was making them feel like a problem to survey rather than a welcome guest in my home. Unable to will the compulsions away I sought a therapist's help and was prescribed medication that I've been taking for the past twenty years. I don't like depending on it, like many of my patients, and feel at times like I should be able to control it on my own, but when I stop taking the drug, my agitation returns as do my relational problems. The agitation has always been there but when it finally went away I had a point of comparison and seeing the difference made the decision an easy one. There's no point in struggling over molehills when treatment enables me to climb mountains.

It's hard to differentiate between what is learned and what is biologically inherited when it comes to any mental illness. Those in the field believe it is a combination of both. I have seen patients who demonstrate Asperger idiosyncrasies without actually meeting the diagnostic criteria. They are often the children of Asperger parents. It is entirely reasonable to expect children to emulate the parent's behaviors, normal or otherwise. The same holds true with OCD. My own experience strongly validates the biological factor as I can feel the compulsions arise in an unforgiving way. They pull like a beast. Miming parents behaviors don't feel the same internally, and seems more flexible in yielding to reality. For example, I learned to walk as though the floor were made of eggshells since my father couldn't bear the sound of footsteps across the room, especially if he was downstairs from me. I still do that today but it is not a compulsion. I don't feel inner chaos if I were to thump heavy-footed across the floor. When it comes to crumbs, however, I can't let it be, I will focus on them unwillingly, unable to let go until they are gone. One feels a choice, the other clearly not.

Research suggests we are genetically predisposed to the disorders and our environments either turn the switch on or not, just like physical illnesses. It's hard to imagine a switch not getting turned on, however, when you have a parent with the illness. Stress is clearly a factor in genetic expression and it often antagonizes the degree of symptomatology.

When Dad was diagnosed, Mom's inability to function became more pronounced. The specialists treating him for his brain cancer urged us to limit treatment to radiation and medication since a final stage glioblastoma is unsurvivable and treatment would impede the quality of life remaining. The surgeon, however, was eager to operate, offering us a few more months. My mother would not make a decision despite the doctors' pressure, my uncle's pleading, and our own urging. Time was an imperative, if he was going to have the surgery they needed to know immediately. Still Mom wouldn't decide. She was in the infamous double-bind without an option she could live with. After our threatening insistence she finally said she would leave it up to my siblings and me.

Making this decision would have been more painful had I not been in a fog at the time. The overwhelm acted as a shutoff valve and the only emotion that found its way to the surface was often anger. Anger at Mom's torturing vacillation between interference and avoidance and her inability to be helpful in any way. When I allowed any feelings to open my heart it broke for her, as well as my father, and that pain could have served as a catalyst to a deeper connection between all of us. But none of us could hold it. Like we did our entire lives we took individual paths in dealing with our grief.

When the doctor called asking me for the family's decision I felt somewhat disoriented in having a conversation of this weight. I am the youngest after all, and by a wide margin, and had always been dismissed as a child even through adulthood. What I thought never held much gravity, especially in Mom's eyes, and now I would be the one to say the words no one wanted to say. The somber facts were clear, while aggressive treatment would perhaps be a good option for us to have Dad a little longer, it was a bad one for him. So I said the words with love and with certainty,

"We decided to pursue palliative care." The doctor sighed in relief, said it was what he would do if it was his parent as well. I hung up the phone, sadly not sharing the doctor's relief, but feeling as though I had just killed my father. This, I thought, was the reason my mother deferred to us, so that we could be the executioners and she could grieve him without guilt. "Okay," I thought, "consider it a gift."

Two days later, still feeling the heaviness of his death sentence I got a call from my uncle saying that Dad's surgery was scheduled for the next morning. "What?" I yelled into the phone. "Well," he said, "your mother heard the word hospice and told the doctor to do the surgery." I felt as though someone had played a cruel joke on me. Had we gone through this for nothing? Had Mom bet on us choosing the surgical option, which was the decision she wanted all along, but one she couldn't sign off on or be responsible for? Was this the pro level of the I want Italian for dinner but let's play the game until you get to the end I want but wont tell you I want? This was by far, her most manipulative plan. I don't think it a fully conscious one, but rather that invisible road map once again, that gets her to and fro without actual decision-making or committing. Point A: I want him to have the surgery but am afraid I will be responsible for his death, to point B: his having the surgery without her deciding. Only we failed to drop into the correct, predetermined slot.

I was not there for Dad's operation, unable to get there in time. When I arrived the next night I entered his hospital room and immediately felt the blood drain from my head, my legs felt made of clumsy springs as I walked drunkenly toward his bed. He was nearly unrecognizable. It looked as though every bit of life was taken from him, my domineering father now a skeletal and vacant being awaiting an inevitable death. This would be my first loss of a close family member and I had been terrified upon hearing his diagnosis, fearful I didn't have the strength to get through the nightmare. Seeing him now confirmed my fear.

Although the surgery was successful in removing most of the tumor and in theory, giving him another six-to-twelve-months, Dad never rebounded. The next two months were filled with a daily diminishing hope. Physical rehab was a disaster and only exhausted his will. He begged for rest. Over the course of weeks we all flew in to take turns visiting and helping Mom. We got through it like all prolonged challenges, an inch at a time. Each heartbreaking moment replacing the last, bolstering themselves up on the last successful breath taken, forging a tolerance of sorts. Dad recovered to some degree, looking healthier, a little more himself, but with a diagonal smile like a slash-mouth emoji, from the stroke. We had conversations as he moved in and out of coherence. Oftentimes he was in the past, a small boy, calling out for his mother. The days were disorienting, without precedence. About two weeks in the improvements stopped. No day was better than the last. He had topped out, plateaued, and then began the decline. He asked to come home. Mom said no. She had her reasons. After a week in the hospital, six weeks in rehab and one week in hospice Dad passed away at eighty-five years old, shortly after Christmas.

Mom had to face the outcome of her decision. The surgery had surely shortened his time with us but we didn't regret it since his death seemed to have saved him more suffering. We did our best to reassure her it was okay, that either decision was agony in the making. We will never know what was the right one in reality but I am immensely grateful he had a painless and fearless death and I can offer my mother that consolation in her decision. Sadly however, the trashing of my gift, in having to make that decision so that she could delegate her guilt, still stings in my heart.

CHAPTER 12
The Not So Fun House

"When loneliness is a constant state of being, it harkens back to a childhood wherein neglect and abandonment were the landscape of life." — *Alexandra Katehakis*

While all relationships are of value and importance, there is none more vulnerable than that of parent and child. A primary caregiver with severe and untreated OCD puts a child at risk for developmental issues. Most adults possess both the internal and external resources to manage the damage done by OCD/mental illness. It may not be ideal, but couples can divorce, family members can distance themselves, and friendships can end. But what are the options available for the children of ill parents?

Neglect is common with OCD parenting. OCD mothers and fathers tend to meet their own obsessive needs first even if they are at the expense of the children. Neglect can occur in many forms, sometimes it's the simple misreading of the child's needs, as OCD sufferers often have difficulty with preoccupation and thus struggle to be present with their children. With my own parent she was often too overwhelmed with her own distress to make space for mine.

A child's self-worth often becomes entwined with the parent's compulsions. Often I felt like the dirt that needed cleaning. In my early days, when snow angels were the delight of childhood, I felt joy in being one with the white mountains in the front yard. Numb fingers and toes couldn't compete with the exuberance of those moments and I'd stay out for hours until they were literally blue. When I finally surrendered and went inside I'd be stopped in the hallway made to stand for inspection on the green linoleum hexagons, whose color was designed but failed to evoke rich green marble, as I dripped not exuberance but gritty water drops on my mother's pristine floor. She saw only the mess I had made, not the joy beneath the mess. I was the bearer of the mess and ultimately I was the mess. I felt that deeply. I was the source of my mother's anger and anxiety and I was a burden to her. I could not see that the problem was the disorder. No one had ever taken the time to explain to us why Mom was always so upset. I only knew from how she looked at me that my existence perturbed her and if I ever had any doubts of this she confirmed it with statements like "I should have become a nun," and "Someday I'm going to burn down this house." Her regrets in having a family were clear, as was her unhappiness. As a child I internalized her rejection of her life and of us, and began to identify with the unworthiness she projected.

OCD is a cunning disorder. It's not overt like growing up around alcohol or drug abuse and yet the experiences are often similar. To the addict, the substance is the priority over everything and everyone and the rationalizations defending the addiction are maddening. Replace drug and/or alcohol with obsession and/or compulsions and you have a very familiar set of symptoms.

Either way it's tremendously painful for a loved one to live so many rungs below in importance and inevitably a power struggle ensues in both types of households. In the argument with an addict, a statement like "If you love me you will not drink tonight," is a pretty reasonable demand, though often futile. With OCD, however, the fight is much less clear, and can seem ridiculous. You can't exactly say, "If you love me you won't wash your hands for the ninetieth time today" and sound reasonable. If your feelings get hurt because Mom is "choosing" her household chores and responsibilities over having lunch together, you will only seem incredibly needy and selfish. The compulsions disguised as responsible behavior, productive and necessary, appear undeserving of complaint and the person complaining begins to look like the problem for being overly reactive to silly things. I can be annoyed at your house checking, your counting numbers out loud, your avoidance of touching the bathroom door in your own house! But at the end of the day it's hard to quantify how any of that is a problem for me personally. The telescope needs to be flipped around to really see the issues, in order to go deeper. For example, my mother could not stomach washing diapers in the pre-Pampers era so she toilet trained all of us at an absurd age. She began putting us on toilets at six months old and by the time we were eighteen months we were completely trained. This is great source of pride for her and when she would tell people they were truly impressed with Mom's determination. For me however, it's likely the reason I've had lifelong digestive issues. I could only imagine her reaction every time I had an inconvenient bowel movement, not that any were likely convenient. It was all just too much and that disgust jumped from her synapses to mine I am certain. Neurons that fire together wire together, this is called the Hebb's Effect and it occurs during emotionally charged experiences as our brains gather up all the simultaneous variables into a neural net in order to help us avoid future harm. If a bee stung my cheek while I was listening to Adele on the radio, I may have an unpleasant physical reaction the next time I hear that song or that artist. Its nature's way of warning me that a bee might be near. If my mother's reaction to a dirty diaper is predictably frenetic and frustrated her baby could begin to associate their natural bodily sensations, such as digestion, with feelings of anxiety. This is a longer and more complex explanation than to say my mother's drunkenness caused me to feel unsafe, which is an obvious concept by comparison.

The fact that no one in our home was conscious enough to truly grasp what was happening drove the suffering underground. I recall Ms. M (my high school guidance counselor) attempting to figure out what was going on with me; I was clearly having problems at home, I was anxious, depressed, and my grades were failing, but I was completely unable to participate in the process. I never mentioned any of these stories to her, despite trusting her. It simply never occurred to me, and if it had it is doubtful that even an experienced and seasoned counselor would have connected the dots between Mom's OCD and my struggles.

Neither Mom nor Dad understood the consequences of Mom's illness. They could not see how it was impacting our relationships or emotional development. While her symptoms openly manifested in ritualistic cleaning and checking, the emotional and psychological impacts were just too covert for any of us to process. Mom certainly couldn't understand how she was hurting me and my reactions to her seemed like immature and unnecessary drama. Her OCD was not ridiculous, I was.

If you were to say to someone that an alcoholic raised you, or a schizophrenic, or manic depressive person, they likely have a sense of what it was like for you growing up. But when you say a parent with OCD raised you they conjure images of a clean house! How bad can that be? Well, I am here to tell you, it can be pretty damn bad and there are no 12-step groups for us as there are for children of alcoholics. There is little information, targeted treatment, advice, or advocacy for children of OCD parents and understanding is a critical part of the healing.

Children of OCD parents may develop problems with anxiety, depression, and their own OCD symptoms.

The OCD parent often indoctrinates the child into the obsessions, compulsions, and/or rituals and there is the likelihood of "catching" them. Relationships may also be challenging since power and control issues often arise in an effort to make sense of the senseless. I frequently got fixated on truths so that Mom couldn't get in there and distort them on me. I grew to be rigidly protective of my feelings and perceptions. Children in OCD households have spent their lifetimes attempting to create order out of a disordered reality. Letting go of control may feel life-threatening at times, since the OCD parent is often incapable of providing safety for them, which is a paradoxical irony since OCD sufferers often obsess about safety and yet they often leave their children defenseless and vulnerable. Mom always worried about things that never happened and rarely worried about things that did. She'd get nearly hysterical about roller coasters but would disregard my coming home drunk at fourteen years old. Children may also develop problems with trust, questioning the true motive of others, and over-analyzing or over-interpreting their intentions. In my experience, Mom loved me in words and sentiment but her behavior didn't feel like love, not in the verb. I began questioning her motives early in my childhood, I didn't feel like her caring for me was about me at all. People with severe OCD often don't say what they mean or mean what they say, but rather tailor their thoughts and comments to manage their guilt and shame. Mom would tell me what she thought I needed to hear, but not how she really felt. She often lied to me to give way to her compulsions, like a child trying to avoid punishment.

Secrecy is common as well. It is easy for children with this kind of modeling and interactive experiences to become confused in discerning what is real, and secrecy may breed anxiety and mistrust. Keeping face is crucial for the OCD parent and secrets safeguard the illusion of the perfect parent and family. When children witness their parents lying in order to cover up their flaws an inherent message is learned, "I am not worthy as I am." My mother taught us not to share our secrets with potential partners, to hide our flaws, and to find someone who would love us more than we love them, to safeguard our hearts. This notion of relational gaming confused me greatly and caused me to question my lovability. It also made me wonder if my mother played by her own rules. Did she not love me as much as I loved her? It reinforced the feeling that I did not truly know who she was beneath her own secrets.

CHAPTER 13
Oven, Stove, Refrigerator

"If we do not transform our pain, we will most assuredly transmit it - usually to those closest to us: our family, our neighbors, our coworkers, and invariably, the most vulnerable, our children." — Father Richard Rohr

The universe does not subscribe to predictability and order, the two warm blankets of life. If only tragedies occurred on set days or were caused by foreseeable threats, we could bypass their inevitability with a quick defensive maneuver and Mom could maybe skip a day of rituals. Sadly our lives don't abide by our need for control despite our best efforts. So Mom can't afford to miss a day of circling the kitchen three times, repeating "oven, stove, refrigerator" while pressing the doors and checking the knobs in order to keep the evil away. Like urgent whispers in a foxhole, she orders, "Closed, off, off, off, closed," thrice around the kitchen.

Mom says she fears leaving the gas on but it goes deeper than that. The stove is the proxy for the world at large, for every conceivable threat that exists in the universe and her ritual of checking is keeping the threats controlled and at bay. Fearing for the safety of loved ones is a full time job and adding new members to the mix seemed imprudent to me; I wondered why she had children to begin with. She said she had a family because it was what was expected, "That's what you did in my time, you got married and had kids." Perhaps she suspected she wouldn't be able to tend to both her compulsions and her children, at least not without a plan, so she decided to space out her pregnancies every five years so that the older kid(s) would be in school when the new ones arrived, which worked the first time but not when I came along.

Mom needed to be done with my birthing so she could focus on getting my two siblings started in the school year. Things needed to be perfect and my sister and brother had to arrive fresh for their first day, meticulously groomed. I suppose she couldn't leave that to my aunt in order to give me proper womb time to develop the neural connections of my brain.

The problem of my due date was that I was due to arrive two weeks after the new school term began, which would be a huge interruption and she couldn't have that. It was a "no limoncello before dinner" kind of chronology in her mind, it makes little sense to me but I had to come before school started and that was that. She told her doctor of her strategy, of having me on the fifth of September, a full two weeks before nature strongly recommended. He was not keen on the idea. He told her she needed to carry as long as possible and reminded her of her history, how my brother and sister were both underweight and she shouldn't even be having a third baby let alone a premature one. This is the part that fills my mother with pride, "I told him no, I need to have it before I send my other two off to school. My baby will come before Labor Day, it will come the fifth, you'll see."

And see he did, I was born on the fifth of September, at five pounds two ounces, her smallest baby yet. Mom was as delighted as the doctor was dismayed. The first time Mom told me the story, I asked how she managed such a feat and she said, "Your mother is clever," smiling smugly, "I pushed my old vacuum around, and moved some heavy furniture and sure enough." Her pride made my jaw clench. "So you had me come early despite the doctor's warning, just because school started?" She just smiled in response, too pleased to hear my agitation. She successfully got us home from the hospital with time to spare and my siblings went to their first day of school freshly bathed in immaculate little outfits, not a hair out of place. How could she not have been proud?

The boastful re-telling of this story on each of my birthdays is a cruel reminder of my place on the OCD food chain. Why wasn't I important enough to be considered? Why hadn't the doctor's cautions concerned her? Didn't she care about the effect on me? The answer is that the part of her brain in which I would matter wasn't in charge. The need to ensure and protect my well-being never made it into consciousness, or if it did, got immediately overshadowed by the needs of this demanding disorder. In another time and place she cared about me tremendously, would "lay down and die" for me as she often would say, but in this moment, with this conflict, my viability was trumped by a compulsion.

These were the things that safeguarded her from the perilous germs on the faucet, HIV atoms flying in the air, and imaginary gas leaks, but her baby's under developed nervous system, not so much. This is my perspective of course, my personal truth, and it's very different from the one she has written for herself. In her reality she had wisely waved off the doctor's concerns with a flip of the hand, he was just silly in worrying. She knew I would be fine. It just made good sense timing wise. She's a great mother with impeccable organization. Our two opposing stories would never evolve or merge but would ever run parallel and separate, like our relationship. The fact was that her very first act as my mother made an indelible mark on me and set the stage for our roles, it was our genesis.

It felt as though time was static in our family as very little changed over the years. Mom's OCD felt like Groundhog Day, each day beginning and ending like the one before. Time wouldn't resolve our problems, but rather solidify them unapologetically. There never seemed any time for evaluation or moments of regret. Mom's disorder was not going anywhere and would be a permanent fixture for which everything around it had to adjust. It would not be confronted, addressed, debated, or even mentioned, but instead accommodated as reflexively as a knee-jerk to a hammer. This was our normal. With no lulls in our saga, there were no opportunities for healing. How can you forgive what is done repetitively and without acknowledgment, insight, or apology?

We rarely went out as Mom didn't drive and so the vast majority of our time together was confined to our home, which could have been cozy like a snow day, but instead felt as sterile as an institution. We had ample opportunity to play, read, do homework, and yet I haven't any memory of doing any activities together. There was not a single experience with Mom out of the house, just her and I. Our days consisted of my staying out of her way as she tirelessly cleaned. She wanted me to help but I wanted no part of it. I did the chores I was required to do and then went out with friends. When I was a freshman in high school we sat one morning at the kitchen table eating breakfast. She was telling me about her dream the night before, which is something she loved to do. She'd practically reenact them, high on the drama. Still, I was often bored by the telling. I wanted Mom to inquire about my own dreams, the ones from last night and the ones for the future. Unlike my friends, I wanted my mother engaged and interested in my life. I yearned for her curiosity about me. Eating my bowl of cereal on this particular morning an impulsive slip escaped me, "Mom, I'd really like it if you asked me about school sometimes." I knew as the words left my lips it was a very bad idea, but there it was out in the space between us, hanging thick in the air like smog. You don't make demands on Mom, even in the most innocuous way. She heard them only as criticisms, or worse, as neediness. I felt the anticipatory rejection rise in my chest and began backing away from the table. It had happened too many times in the past not to be gun-shy, times when I'd finally reach across the abyss and attempt to connect only to wind up in a free fall. Like the time when I regretfully took the advice of my fourth grade teacher Mrs. Fenishell who, as she wiped tears from my face, coached me to tell my mother that I was sad she had given my favorite doll to my neighbor. I didn't think my poor naive teacher had a grasp of what I was up against but I gave it my best shot nonetheless. That night I kissed Mom good night as she rested on the sofa watching television and did just as I'd been instructed. "Mom," I said, "I was really sad you gave Nina my favorite doll. It really hurt my feelings." She looked back at me as though I uttered sheer nonsense. She was tired, exhausted from her labors of the day, "Oh Juliane, stop being so ridiculous, you never even play with dolls, it sat in your closet forever, just go to bed." The next day Mrs. F asked how it had gone. "Great!" I lied, "Mom said she was sorry." In all of my eight years Mom had never apologized for anything, it was not in her vernacular in any of her relationships. She was incapable of accepting her mistakes, which were an absolute threat to her constant need for perfection. So I lied to my teacher caring more about her feeling helpful than I did about my own disappointment and shame.

So I know from experience how this breakfast conversation will end but sometimes biting my tongue just isn't an option and words find their way out of my mouth.

Sometimes they even come from hope. But sitting across from Mom now I was already regretting the impulse. I wished I could erase the words she would hear as a fault exposed, despite my use of the overrated "I" statement.

Mom has this way of holding her head when her righteous pride gets activated, it turns off to the side, stretching her neck like a slingshot ready to fire. So when her chin shifted right I prepared myself, "You know how hard I work around this house. You see how tired I am. I'm too busy, I just don't have the time to do anything else. Today it's the plumber coming. Your father knows I hate having workmen come through this house, they leave mud on the floor, and I just cleaned them for God's sake. One of these days I'm just going to burn this damn house down, I'm so sick of being everyone's slave," she said in a single breath. I had heard this particular psalm many times before, I knew what was queuing up next and before she could continue I barked, "Mom, God I just want you to ask me a question, forget it." She looked at me resentfully; I am unappreciative and spoiled, in her mind, a brat. "Fine" she says, "I'll tell you what, you do some chores around this house and I will ask you about school." She couldn't be serious, and yet her eyes said otherwise, revealing a victor's gloat. I don't think she expected my response when I said, "Okay, you have a deal."

We made the agreement and even signed a contract that day, my promising to clean her beloved plastic tree, dust the furniture, vacuum the rugs, and make my bed, and in return she would show interest in my schooling.

The next day Mom gave me a lesson on how to dust that dreadful plastic tree in the living room, leaf by leaf, with a wet paper towel. She was very serious about how to wipe them from end to end, to be sure to change the paper towel once it was dirty and get the leaves in the back that were hard to reach. I tried to make it fun for myself but there was no joy in this task and I hated every moment of it, but I was also determined. To me it seemed incredibly ridiculous to do this weekly, as if anyone in their right mind would care to notice. But I did it just like she showed me until each and every leaf was bright green again. I had to admit it looked pretty good and if this is what floats her boat who am I to judge. When I was done, I moved on to hoist archaic vacuum out of the closet. Most kids don't enjoy household chores but being a tomboy, I really abhorred them. So I was grateful when I was finally done and could go throw my pinky ball against the house, feeling good about my success, until I caught sight of Mom in the living room, bent over the tree, cleaning it again, leaf by leaf, just as I had done. In the quickest of moments, a feeling of complete deflation overcame me. What was I thinking? Had I really been this naive? What the hell was the point? What was the point of any of it, I thought? There is no middle ground with Mom, no place to ever truly meet. I felt hopeless and betrayed in knowing once again that I would never be good enough and her OCD world would never include me.

The realization that a cleaning partner is not what she truly wanted, that my help would never relieve her burden or give her the extra time she continuously complained about not having, led to my conclusion that two miserable people were certainly not better than one. I raised my white flag and surrendered my need for Mom to be involved in my life. It was done.

A lot of kids in the 70's were vastly independent. Our parents weren't big believers of catering to children. Most of us running the streets were untethered a good amount of time, free to explore wherever we wanted. My childhood didn't have any structure or clearly defined rules. Whatever caused Mom anxiety was prohibited, all else was of no concern. It was as though ignorance truly was bliss and we played a mutual game of don't ask, don't tell. But Mom had certain things that did frighten her, like smoking, dirt, and disease. These things she would ask about again and again, sometimes smelling my fingers to make sure I hadn't had a cigarette, all the while my drinking alcohol at twelve and using drugs not long after never hit her radar. Rules were very confusing to me as were the machinations of Mom's mind. Very little made sense. We simply knew we couldn't rely on her and it wasn't something we ever did, for anything. We were on our own, like miniature adults, and if something bad were to happen, it would be up to us to figure it out, and if anyone was going to need soothing it would also be on us.

Mom was rarely in control of crisis type situations. Besides not having the logistic means such as a driver's license and any degree of physical strength, also absent was a clear head for problem solving. More often she simply made matters worse, more dramatic and exaggerated. When I was fifteen years old I had gotten a bad case of mononucleosis and was housebound for eight weeks. It was a bittersweet time for me because Mom loves to take care of helpless people, it's like a captive audience for her, and I got to lie on the couch, out of her way as she cleaned around me. Every now and then she'd come in, kiss my cheek, and feed me, sometimes even visit. We both look upon this time with affection because it was the most we had ever really connected.

Well into my convalescence we got a call from our nine-year-old neighbor Nina who had gotten news that her older sister Denise had been hit by a car. Her mother wasn't home and couldn't be reached and she didn't know what to do. My mother went into an immediate panic. I asked what had happened and she told me that my friend Denise still lay in the street, a few blocks away. My mother was no better at crisis than the child, all she could do was spit out question after question, yelling, and crying hysterically. I ran to my room, threw on a pair of jeans and in my pajama shirt and winter coat, ran out the door. It was October in New York and I hadn't been outside the house in weeks. It was a raw fall day and the cold air pierced my lungs immediately. I didn't know how I would make it four blocks when I got breathless walking back and forth to the bathroom, but I had no choice. I started a slow trot with visions of what I would find once I got to her, was she still alive? Would there be a lot of blood? Would she be able to speak? My legs quickened their pace, I had better hurry, as much for Denise as for the unhinged woman I left at home. As I ran sharp and shooting pain quickly began attacking my left flank, jabbing at me with pitchforks. The doctors had said the virus inflamed my spleen. I didn't know exactly where or what a spleen was but I was pretty sure it was angry. I was only a block in and I already feared my legs would buckle. Still I ran as fast as my body would allow, panting hot breath into the cold damp air. Rounding the third block I could see ahead at what looked like cars stranded in haphazard positions, one facing this way, another facing that, as though abandoned. There were people kneeling in the middle of this major boulevard, some in uniforms, some obvious passersby. As I got closer I saw a yellow chalk mark outlining a body, her body, and I feared the worst. When I finally reached her I bent over, gasping for air; I wondered if I might have to join her in the ambulance. Looking down I squinted, as though trying to limit the full impact of what I might see. Her face looked the same, and I was able to breathe a moment of relief. The friend with whom I had shared most of my early memories, played with since I was two years of age, who I had shared a bed with so that I too could get the mumps, who taught me how to add, subtract, and use fancy words, lay there motionless, expressionless, almost serene. The paramedics asked if I knew her, and I told them yes, like a sister. At the sound of my voice, Denise suddenly opened her eyes, wide and crazed, and immediately began screaming my name, so grateful to see a familiar face, maybe even to see my specific face. I bent my stiff knees, and sat on the cold ground beside her as she squeezed my hand with great strength. I was immune to the pain of her grip, aware only of the relief I felt in the fact that her muscles maintained their might. In my peripheral vision I could see that her leg was badly mangled and the contortion of her body made me fear she might never walk again.

Feeling the split of needing to be in two places at one time, I tried to triage who and what was needed more, my friend's comfort or Mom's management. As if reading my mind Denise pulled my hand closer to her body and pleaded for me to stay with her. I knew the more minutes that passed the more frightened and out-of-control Mom would become. She would need someone to calm her crazy, at the very least provide a status update, and this was not the time of cell phones. I feared she'd be hysterical by this point, even more than when I left her and the idea of her being alone made me feel sick. But there was no real contest in who needed me more, so I tucked the bottom of my parka beneath my butt and got comfortable. Mom would have to make do.

When the ambulance took my friend away I ran back, stopping first to check on Nina. She must be so frightened and alone and the least I could do was let her know her sister was alive. I ran again against the cold wind, turning the corner to her house. I slow hopped the porch steps and landed breathless at the front door, looking straight at... Mom. Opening the screen door for me, she was indeed more hysterical than when I had left her and now had Nina in the grips of her panic.

Upon seeing me, the nine-year-old began screaming and wailing inconsolably with my mother simultaneously echoing her. She had doubled down on my task. Despite feeling exhausted and weakened, I had to repress my own fear and the vision of my friend mangled and torn. "Mom" I yelled, "what are you doing? This is how you help? You've scared this poor kid half to death, just stop it," I ordered. I've become my father's soldier, taking control of situations like these, just as he had. And just as she had responded to him, she was resistant to heed any commands. I didn't know of a way to soothe her that wouldn't break me further. I could not summon any type of softness or compassion, because that was a foreign experience in my home. When you cried, Dad told you that you had made your bed now you must sleep in it and Mom would jump in the well with you and become the one needing soothing. To comfort her with patience and care now would have just enraged me more. So instead I barked, like Dad.

That night when Dad got home we all sat together in the living room decompressing from the ordeal. Denise's leg was in bad shape and she would require several surgeries. It would be a long rehabilitation but she would be okay. The adrenaline had finally quit its surge and I felt spent like never before. I am sure I needed something from my parents, but I didn't know what, and neither did they. Ten days later I returned to school. I told Ms. M about what had happened. I told her my friend was okay and she looked at me very seriously, and asked, "Well what about you, are you okay?" "I don't know," I replied, no one had asked, including myself, and it hadn't occurred to me that I might not be. "Well," she said, "you may not have been lying on the ground like your friend but you've been through a lot. And you were essentially on your own having to manage everything." "Yeah, I suppose," I said, not feeling the weight of her words. "Well maybe you can talk to your parents about how you felt and how it's still affecting you," she offered. "Yeah maybe," I shrugged, grateful for her caring but knowing I would never fall for that advice again.

CHAPTER 14
A Thorn in the Paw

"The saddest thing about betrayal is that it never comes from your enemies." —Unknown

We never get so old that we don't still want our mother's love and support. That is why we may trick ourselves into hoping its not too late, that one day we may even share an experience in which real connection occurs. Today, I shared a conversation with Mom that I'd had with my Uncle because, while she loves my dad's brother, she knows how difficult he can be and how his silent treatment can be infuriating and hurtful. So I thought maybe she could empathize.

"So Uncle Charlie won't talk to me."

"What? Why?"

"No clue. I called there last week and he refused to get on the phone. Aunt Dot said, 'Charlie, Juliane's on the phone, want to pick up?' and he yelled out an emphatic 'No!'."

Mom looks distressed by this and I am hopeful for a moment that she is on my side. "Maybe he's mad I didn't send him a Christmas card" (this has been eating at her all month. She doesn't make the effort and then perseverates with guilt and projection).

"Mom, he's mad at me not you."

"Well, if he's mad at you maybe he's mad at me too since I didn't send him a card."

"No, I don't think so, he spoke to you last time you called and always takes your call. I'm talking about me."

"You know he was this way with your father, refusing to talk to him, all because Dad said Jimmy (his son) was fat. He's moody that way. You know my family was never like that, holding grudges. Well, my brothers Johnny and Freddie had a falling out but that was about business. But really it was their wives. When one got a mink coat the other asked "why don't I have one too?" See your mother was never like that, I never needed a mink coat. I never needed things like that but of course your father had to get me one. I don't even know where it is now."

Exhausted from the tangential jaunt, I surrender, "You know Mom I was just trying to tell you about my experience, about me."

"Well, what did you do, that he's so mad?"

She looks away in silence and has nothing else to say.

What did the child inside want? To be loved, seen, heard, and known, of course. It was a basic need at work, so basic most anyone would have answered it easily enough. What would have been so difficult in saying, "I'm so sorry, I know how close you and your uncle are. He was always like a father to you, that is so hurtful." Any response to show concern, compassion, understanding, or validation would have been like Christmas morning to this child who simply wanted comfort from her mother. But this is not who my mother is, she is unable to see beyond her own reflection. If my uncle was angry with me, it was because of her. This seems on the surface self-deprecating but in actuality it is a negative inflation, with an emphasis on inflation. All things are about her, because of her, happening to her.

It might be difficult to see the connections to her OCD but when you consider how shame works it becomes more obvious. The reason compulsions and rituals exist is to protect from shameful thoughts, feelings and actions. Compulsive washing works out feelings of guilt, in essence cleansing oneself, while also providing a haven of distraction. The worse her conscience feels, the greater the need to escape from it. What looks like narcissistic self-focus is really the psyche's attempt to screen for the smallest "wrongness."

So back to the conversation about Uncle Charlie. When Mom hears he is upset she jumps to shame and defensiveness. Her system responds with an automatic "Uh oh, I did something bad and wrong," or worse, "I am bad and wrong." It doesn't matter that I said he was angry with me. She feels guilty about not sending a Christmas card so that is the limit of her focus. I am irrelevant. The OCD brain cannot handle an infraction to perfection so it is strategizing a response, attempting to shed itself of any perceived wrongness. It cannot digest mistakes. After one particularly horrific fight in which she adamantly refused to own her actions and apologize she said she would rather die. I couldn't believe what I was hearing, so I sought to clarify what clearly was a misunderstanding, even she wasn't this rigid. I asked incredulously "So you would rather kill yourself than be wrong?" to which she responded with a glaring, "Yes, I would rather be dead than wrong."

An understanding of how and why our conversation about Uncle Charlie evolved requires an appreciation of this irrational mindset. The statement "I am not like my sisters-in-law, I don't need a mink coat and in fact I don't even know where mine is" seems like it came out of thin air, completely random and unexpected. However, it is quite integral to the equation. The memory is selected like a super sonic speed check through her personal card catalog of experiences, found under the heading of "GOOD" and cross referenced with: self-effacement, martyrdom, humility, and innocence. Her indifference to the mink coat, the very thing women craved in a distasteful superficiality was of no importance to her whatsoever ergo, "I want for nothing, and cannot possibly be seen as bad." If I hadn't interrupted the spiel it would have gone on indefinitely, pulling out one card after another n support of her irreproachability. But disappointingly for her, my tolerance rarely exceeds twenty minutes before that all too familiar feeling of invisibility takes over and I have to stop her. It starts with a sinking sensation, followed by one of shrinking from the inside. It's as though my body is becoming infinitesimally smaller, until finally I disappear, evaporated on the spot, a drop of water on a hot pan.

That is the nature of triggers, they are tricky little bastards that hide in the fields, waiting for that unsuspecting foot to take its next step. To the outsider it is a silly and senseless provocation, "Grow up, get over it," exaggerated and indulgent, but to the victim, it is a gun, locked and loaded. Triggers are stubborn and rarely apt to heal completely so we had better get good at dealing with them. One alternative to constant re-victimization is learning to map the land mines, and navigate with increasingly better GPS, steering clear when we are able. We need to remember their presence within us, like an arthritic knee that acts up in damp weather. We stay aware of our needs, and the places in which we are exposed and in time we get better at protecting ourselves, at self-parenting our wounded child, keeping her safe from further harm, and then those triggers will finally begin to lose their potency. They will still react, but more as rain showers than typhoons.

I am highlighting the point here that time is not enough. These old wounds will not heal on their own, just as infections will eventually spread if not treated. In the 12-step program they talk about the dry drunk, a name for those who quit using but who don't work the steps in order to address the triggers of the addiction. They consider themselves sober but their "-ism," a.k.a. their disease, is still running the show. When I hear people say that the past is better left in the past

I think of the dry drunk, who has stopped drinking without working the program, continuing the negative behaviors associated with the drinking. We may act like we are no longer affected by the past and that we barely even think of it, and yet we are raging lunatics in traffic and worse yet, we wind up passing down a psychological inheritance to our children. Our old wounds will find a dysfunctional way out if not functionally worked out.

Yes, these experiences are painful, and yes they derail us from our otherwise content lives so it is rational to want to avoid and reject them when they intrude upon us. But in turning against these unwanted feelings we, in essence, reject ourselves, especially the most hurt and vulnerable parts, and most often the wounded child within us. Imagine punishing a frightened child by locking her in a dark closet. That is what we do to ourselves when we push aside our feelings because they are uncomfortable or embarrassing. We add a horrible and unnecessary layer to our suffering. Often clients tell me that they respond to their fear with shame, their jealousy with judgment, their selfishness with hate. We think that by engaging in these negative self-appraisals we hold ourselves to a higher standard, putting an end to bad behaviors. If I hate myself for these things then I will strive to be a better person. That was certainly the belief of previous generations. Withhold love and approval and you will create motivation for hard work and strong character. If we offer love and kindness toward bad behavior we will create a spoiled and selfish child. Research shows that shame is an obstacle to learning. It is when we feel most safe and loved that we are most available to focus and motivation, and we are naturally driven to want to live up to praise when we get it rather than risk losing it. And we will likely experience fear and performance anxiety when love is conditional upon success. When we apply this faulty kind of parenting to ourselves we experience similar psychological problems. Our negative self-appraisals and shaming cause us to shrink from our most wonderful potential and we begin to fear taking risks. But rather when we are gentle with our inevitable flaws and imperfections and meet our doubts and emotional discomforts with patience and kindness, the same way we would with a child in pain, we are open to compassion and healing.

The self-soothing process is a critically important function in the journey of healing therefore it requires time and attention in its development. When we fail in self-tending and instead reject our internal experiences, we repeat the cycle of injury. The unresolved wounds are those that didn't receive adequate love and attention in the first place, and by withholding from ourselves those same things, we strengthen the trauma. When we don't respond to a crying infant he will scream with greater volume and intensity, and if he is ignored still, he will eventually give up, which is an apocalyptic event in terms of psychic development. Neglect often sets the mold for how individuals relate to themselves, the world, and their own needs. They may learn that they are unworthy of love, and that their needs are irrelevant. If this happens, an individual may not know what it is they need because they are no longer conscious of it. It's as if the need says, "Why bother, no one is coming anyway."

We need, therefore, to build a solid and caring relationship with our pain and our darkness, befriending them in a way we would someone we love and value unconditionally. We don't shame our closest friends or summon our children to the closet when they hurt but rather meet them with curiosity and compassion. Sometimes my patients have a hard time with this, feeling like they are blocked from feeling empathy for themselves or for the child inside. Many believe they are undeserving of that kind of nurturing, or that compassion will fuel the inadequacies by enabling or pacifying them. While I'm not a religious person per se, I look to the teachings of Jesus as an example of how to have relationships with, not only others, but with ourselves. He responds to the gravest of sins with neither punishment nor judgment, but rather compassion and forgiveness. Just before his death his plea to his Father is for a pardon of his executioners. If we can practice forgiveness for ourselves then we can open up to love again. Condemnation on the other hand breeds self-hatred which, in turn, extends to our neighbors like brush fire. Jesus, I believe, understood that chain effect.

Author, psychologist, and Buddhist teacher Tara Brach talks about the two wings of mindfulness—awareness and compassion. I remind my patients that unless we practice both wings we would be better off not doing the work at all. Building insight into ourselves can reveal some very dark truths since human beings are all inherently flawed and while the insights are important to teach us a lesson, reshape our belief systems, and guide future behavior, they can also cause us to feel deep shame and self-loathing. When we become aware of these parts of ourselves it is necessary that we extend compassion to what we find, to be curious about its role, and to find the thorn in the lion's paw.

There is never a shortage of opportunities to practice this work. It is a lifelong journey. The most common thing I hear from patients is their wish for a different problem, anything, just not the same one they come up against over and over again. I can relate to their frustration and sense of futility. We begin to doubt we will ever put our wounds behind us. One of the most pervasive triggers for me is Mom's denial of the past. My siblings and I have distinct memories of Dad getting physically aggressive and even violent with us. I am continually perplexed at how often the subject arises, over five decades and still counting. I have begun to wonder if Mom has an unconscious need to repeat this process of confrontation/denial for whatever reasons. It goes something like this:

"My friend Dolores had it so bad as a child. Her father was so abusive he even hit her," Mom says in disbelief.

"That's terrible, truly."

"I just don't understand how a parent can do that to a child. I felt so bad for her." I nod in agreement.

"I mean who does that to their own child?"

I am trying with all my might not to take the bait. Mom is looking at me for a response. I shrug my shoulders.

"And her mother didn't even do anything, she just let him be so cruel." Bingo. Trigger ignited.

"I mean my father was strict, but he never hit us. He never laid a hand on us," she says.

"That must have been nice," I say, finally poking her back.

"What?"

"Your father never hitting you. Must have been nice to feel safe in your own home."

"Well, of course. What are you saying?"

"I'm saying that having a father who never laid a hand on you was fortunate and I wish I could say the same."

"Oh, well your father never hit you kids."

"Say what?"

"Well, he never actually hit you, like with a closed fist. He got mad sometimes but…"

"Are you kidding?"

"No, why would I be kidding? I never let your father hit you."

"No, he didn't hit us with a closed fist, since you prohibited him from that after he gave you a black eye. Leave no marks. Right? That was the rule. So that's okay right? Not bad like your friend Dolores?"

"I don't know what you're talking about, I have no memory of his ever doing that."

"But you have memories of him doing it to you. How is it you remember your own abuse but not ours?"

"Well, he did hit me years ago."

"Yes, and you threw his clothes out onto the lawn and threatened to divorce him. Then you called your brother to straighten him out. He never hit you again, but he turned his rage on us. Only when he did it to us, suddenly you didn't have options, couldn't leave, or get us help. Instead of throwing his clothes out you washed them like nothing happened."

"Well, I don't know what to tell you."

"Well, a simple 'I'm sorry that happened' would mean a lot. Maybe show me some of the compassion you show your friend."

"Well, I just don't remember it that way."

And so it goes, and goes again. We can loop around this way for an hour until it gets so emotionally distressing that I want to punch a wall and she feigns a pending heart attack, neither of which actually happens. Rather we walk away and forget it in a day or two. Nothing ever gets resolved. She won't give me the validation and I, in turn, won't give her the forgiveness.

It angered me that Mom was always behind Dad's outbursts. She called him at work complaining about us, that we were this and we were that. I don't remember what this and that were but certainly nothing to warrant his reactions. By the time he got home from his long day, his pump had been primed and he was eager to unleash on us. At 6'2" inches tall he seemed larger than life, with black beady eyes glaring at us from above, an eagle soaring down upon its prey. He terrified me. This man who was my best friend, who I was more like than anyone else in the family, would morph from being my best champion to my most hateful enemy. His face, long and skinny like the rest of his 170 pound body, contorted with disgust for me, sickened by the sight of me. He hadn't needed to say a single word, or posture whatsoever, his hate for me was enough to crush my heart.

Jung states that it is the "non-doing" that traumatizes us more than the actual events we recall. It's those things we didn't get as children that often impacts us the most. In psychology we differentiate simple trauma from complex trauma. Simple trauma is when we have an event in which we felt powerfulness and threatened with potential harm. Hurricane Katrina victims, for example, experienced simple trauma. The experience is clear, we know exactly what happened. With complex trauma the person may be equally threatened but the underlying cause is not easily identifiable. Often it is relational in nature. As children we know our lives depend upon the love and care of others so when that is at risk, we experience it as trauma. As adults, verbal, mental, and emotional abuse often falls into this category as well. Our physical lives are not necessarily under threat but our psychological survival is at risk. Complex trauma is more difficult in terms of treatment than that of simple trauma because it requires a good deal of investigation.

Because OCD is insidious, it acts as a phantom threat

to families. Like I mentioned earlier, when you are a child of an alcoholic it's pretty clear what is wrong and you can zero in on the experiences more readily. By definition, Dad's rages can be categorized as simple traumas while Mom's role in them complex (relational) traumas. Interestingly, I have been able to forgive Dad in much less time, as the map was much clearer. I knew what needed forgiving. My personal injury list with Mom was much harder to make. She had played the innocent so convincingly and after all it wasn't she who was banging my head against the wall. It took quite a bit of therapy to finally understand how her passivity affected me as complex trauma and to finally begin the work on healing them.

Chapter 15
Meryl's story

"Our wounds are often the openings into the best and most beautiful part of us." —David Richo

I'd like to share an example of the work we do to unknot the present from the past and begin to use new ways of being in our relationships and lives. A client I'll refer to as Meryl recently shared with me a very upsetting childhood memory of her mother becoming extremely angry with her. She described an experience in which she had been frightened when a strange man approached her at the bar her mother had brought her to. Meryl's aunt, who witnessed the inappropriate attention of the man, demanded that her sister take her daughter home. Once home Meryl tried to explain how afraid she felt but instead of consoling her nine-year-old child, her mother angrily blamed her for ruining her good time.

Meryl has many memories of being left alone, often waking up to find her mother gone. There were frequent male visitors to her house after her parents had divorced, and Meryl never felt like she was a priority in her mother's life. Unfortunately her father didn't offer much more in terms of care, often shaming her for her emotions and being overly critical of her interests. Meryl describes her parents using her as a pawn against each other which made her feel guilty and torn. Loving one parent felt like a betrayal of the other.

Meryl's mother likely had a personality disorder as she was frequently neglectful, manipulative, and irresponsible in all of her relationships. However, the family had never addressed the mother's problem or identified it as such. No one had taken the time with Meryl to explain to her that her mother's behavior was due to a problem the mother had, and not because of her.

Sitting in my office Meryl wept as she described feeling like the cause of her mother's unhappiness and anger. Growing up, she felt like a burden and too much for her mother. Meryl has struggled her entire life with identifying and articulating her needs. When she first began seeing me, two years prior, she was unable to connect her childhood experiences to her present day problems. She could not express anger at her parents despite severe neglect, rejection, and manipulative behavior. Her siblings, who are several years older, and who grew up in an entirely different environment, told her she was overly sensitive and that she needed to move on, to "let go of the past already." As a result, Meryl believed that there must be something inherently wrong with her and turned her anger against herself. As years went by, this repressed self-loathing began spilling over into her relationships and she began expressing her anger outwardly.

Meryl's husband Nick is not adept at communication or expressing his feelings. He has his own childhood wounds, struggles with anxiety, and has control issues. Although he loves his wife, he fails to do or say the right thing when it comes to Meryl's needs. He is perplexed as to how to make her happy. As he is frequently preoccupied and overly focused on tasks, Meryl often feels ignored and unappreciated. Like she had growing up with her father, she describes feeling invisible and as though no one hears her. And despite wanting to leave the relationship, she continued to hold the expectations of a committed and intimate couple. While Nick very often failed to say or do something that was loving or caring, everything he actually did held tremendous power over her as if she were an instrument for his playing. All her problems, in her mind, were rooted in him.

Recently Meryl has begun to realize her own role in her relational conflicts and how old beliefs have dictated the course of her experiences. In identifying her underlying assumption of, "I don't deserve to be treated well, respected, or loved" she can see how it has manifested into reality. Accustomed to mixed messages versus assertive communication, Meryl would unknowingly convey a sense of ambiguity and ambivalence when asking for what she needs, often setting herself up to be dismissed. She would come to realize that people failed to take her seriously because she failed to take herself seriously. Consciously she wanted love, attention, and respect, but unconsciously she hadn't believed she deserved it.

Meryl's progress through the healing process has been remarkable. It takes a good deal of courage to face our wounds, as well as a committed willingness to look inside despite what we might find there. Courage is not a lack of fear but rather a moving through the fear. Meryl brought plenty of apprehension into her sessions and her openness was subject to her moods, which were often volatile. But she persevered, showing up even when she was angry with the process or me or both, or even doubtful that the work was worth it. There were even times when she feared she would be annihilated by the work altogether, that she would have a break down from which she'd never recover. Sometimes she didn't want to come in because she was still upset from the week prior. But she always showed up, sometimes open and ready to do the work, and sometimes guarded and defended, but never unwilling to see what might be around the next corner. She never lost hope completely and that is often enough to make it through the hardest parts.

A challenge in working with adult children of any kind of mental illness is helping them to feel their anger. They are often loyal to a fault, reluctant to see the parents through any lens of failure, criticism, or rejection. Typically their role has been one of defense and protection and any straying from that role feels wrong and shameful. The experience of parentification, mentioned earlier, causes the child to feel a deep sense of responsibility and obligation and if there is something wrong with the parent they need protection and care, not criticism and blame.

Even clients who acknowledge their neglect and abuse still have difficulty in owning their anger. There is a noticeable disconnect between their thoughts and emotions, often feeling numb and detached from their own stories. Convincing them that they are entitled to their pain is a process in itself. When Meryl and I first met, I was intrigued by the dichotomies she presented, appearing fragile and vulnerable, yet fierce and combative. Her defenses made an appearance right out of the gate. She was quick in letting me know when I had failed to meet an expectation or hurt her feelings, and her emotional expressions were raw and unbridled.

During the first few months Meryl tested me in all kinds of ways, particularly pushing my boundaries. It is common for people with mentally ill parents to have had their own boundaries violated and although they assume they want to break through the limits of the therapeutic relationship, they are unconsciously seeking reassurance that they will hold even when under pressure. Structure affords clarity and predictability, two traits crucially missing from their childhood. She would call me after hours or when I was on vacation, often in crisis and in emotional turmoil.

There are therapists who will not stretch the limits whatsoever with clients, setting strong boundaries from the get go, refraining from any type of contact between sessions, other than scheduling issues. I personally have found that contracting to use the privilege mindfully and respectfully is usually enough to maintain a safe balance of connection and separateness. I generally tell my clients that I am last on the list of options, but I am certainly on it. I guide and encourage them to use their resources first, both internal and external, reaching out to loved ones when needed. My goal is always to dissuade dependency, to create resiliency and autonomy, and to never throw people into the deep end before they can swim; and some clients simply do not have anyone to support them. So we worked on our boundary setting a little at a time, as I accepted her calls, coached her to calmness as she was having a panic attack on the freeway, and listened empathetically when she was too wounded to get up off the closet floor. A few months into the process we talked about her postponing her calls until after first attempting to self-regulate her emotions, using breathing, self-coaching, distractions, yoga, and engaging in a protocol in reducing panic via sensory awareness.

Panic attacks occur because we are not present. Our mind has been hijacked by an imagined threat which is past-induced or future-looking. When we focus on our sensory experiences we come into the present moment, which unlike the past and future is something we can influence right now. Bringing a focused attention to a tactile, auditory, visual, olfactory, or tasting sensation brings us back into presence. For example, feeling the steering wheel under your fingers, sensing the firm smoothness of the rubber, taut yet yielding, we are engaging our tactile sense which activates our prefrontal cortex. This is the part of the brain that is the manager, in charge of our executive functioning and capable of deescalating irrational fear. The amygdala and hippocampus on the other hand are in charge of our evolutionary protection, ensuring we survive external threats. Unfortunately they can be overreactive, overprotective, and quite wiggy in their usefulness. It is our old brain after all, the one we needed in prehistoric and predatory days and since we are unlikely to be charged by a dinosaur in the near future it causes more unnecessary anxiety than it offers protection.

Meryl has become quite adept at employing these skills, and can generally self-generate enough relief to get through the anxiety on her own. I have not received a crisis call from her in over a year. Some days she will come in and say proudly "I almost called you but didn't," recognizing her own progress.

Once Meryl and I established some limits in our working relationship and she was able to utilize her emotion regulating skills, she began to trust in both me and the process. I had spent several sessions explaining to Meryl the reasons for setting boundaries with her, and that it was difficult to step away sometimes but I did so because I was on her side, waiting and wishing for her own inner hero to arrive. Without this self-disclosure and personal sharing, I risked adding to her history of rejection, abandonment, and confusion. When clients understand that boundaries are set to protect them and safeguard their well-being, versus acting as a random and authoritative exercise of power, they are better able to accept the boundaries with a sense of love and care. This I believe motivates them to honor the limits set and view them as opportunities to cultivate self-love and respect.

After many months of very difficult work we had successfully set a strong foundation of trust and were ready to begin the next level of the process—confronting patterns of behavior that were creating suffering in her life. Without the first part of the work I would not have been able to give Meryl the necessary feedback, her ego was too fragile and defensive. She was unable to separate objective criticism from shaming rejection and resisted a nonjudgmental stance in any way. If I told her that something she did or said was part of the problem she equated this with rejection and blame and assumed I no longer liked or cared about her. Her fear of abandonment would get triggered by the slightest hints of criticism. Words were extremely powerful for her and if I didn't use the right ones she'd lose the entire thread of the work and regress to her childhood shame.

Again I needed to use limited personal disclosure to ensure transparency, which ensures understanding, which ensures trust. I shared with her how difficult it was to talk to her openly and honestly due to her defensiveness, which often evolved into an attack. I explained how my walking on eggshells might help in the moment but would cause bigger problems down the road. I was able to tell her this because she knew that this did not preclude my care, love, and respect for her. It was tremendously painful for her to hear my feedback but the determination in her eyes said, "This will not kill me!"

It took many hours of dialogue about how love, relationships, and life were not black and white concepts and that nothing is all one thing or the other. We practiced using the word "and" in substitution of "but" to remind her that two opposing truths can exist at one time. Making statements such as "I love you and I'm upset you ignored me this morning" seemed like a revelation to her and helped her to accept these dueling realities. In time she was able to trust that while I was the witness to her darkness, I could also contain it without rejecting her. By witnessing her own ability to simultaneously feel love and disappointment, she began to accept the possibility that she could be both wrong and loved.

One of the problems Meryl has with her husband is that he doesn't talk to her about serious issues, or trust her with asking for help. I showed her how in my own experience I hesitated in sharing my thoughts because I sensed she couldn't tolerate the discomfort they might provoke. These were the types of self-disclosures that eventually led to her openness for feedback. She detested the idea that people treated her like a land mine and was motivated to build her tolerance to hearing the truth. We coached her ego in its ability to take a hit, that criticism only felt like it would kill her and not actually do so. Learning that she can be more than one thing at a time helped her to accept some of the inevitable darkness we all have, and to have faith that she was still worthy of love.

The play Wicked is a beautiful example of the dark/light perversion. We assume the Wicked Witch of the West is inherently evil, quick to cause pain and suffering to poor innocents while her sister Glinda, the good witch, is all light and love all of the time. As a prequel to the Wizard of OZ, a very different story unfolds. The evil witch began as an innocent herself, openhearted and true. Glinda on the other hand refuses to embody any of the darkness inherent in our humanity, and is instead stubbornly steadfast in her whimsical fantasy. She repels the pain necessary for integration. In denying her own evil potential it tragically morphs into a projection, landing on her undeserving sister who contains it for her, in essence accepting the role of bad witch.

Evil is born from the seed of denial. Therefore it is essential for each of us to accept our own dark potentials, allowing them a home in which they may integrate with our human goodness. Meryl and I discuss this concept often, as a reminder of our responsibility in carrying our own demons.

Carl Jung emphasizes the importance of keeping our darkness conscious to ensure the evolution of human morality, "Unfortunately there can be no doubt that man is, on the whole, less good than he imagines himself or wants to be. Everyone carries a shadow, and the less it is embodied in the individual's conscious life, the blacker and denser it is. If inferiority is conscious, one always has a chance to correct it…. But if it is repressed and isolated from consciousness, it never gets corrected."

From a spiritual perspective Rumi, a 13th century poet, scholar, and mystic shares this concept beautifully, "This being human is a guest house. Every morning is a new arrival. A joy, a depression, a meanness, some momentary awareness comes as an unexpected visitor...welcome and entertain them all. Treat each guest honorably. The dark thought, the shame, the malice...meet them at the door laughing, and invite them in. Be grateful for whoever comes, because each has been sent as a guide from beyond."

Facing our demons is courageous but accepting them also requires an act of kindness. We need to remember that our humanity guarantees our dark potentials and they are not for the judging or ostracizing but for the compassion and forgiveness. In his book The Art Of Living, Vietnamese Buddhist monk and prolific author Thich Nhat Hanh offers a story of how we can cultivate compassion even for the perpetrators of the most horrific actions. Hearing of the rape and murder of a very young girl and the murder of her father when he tried to save her, as they attempted to escape Vietnam by boat, he describes being overcome by anger and sadness. He then describes his work, through meditation and mindfulness, to put himself deeply into the shoes of the perpetrator. He saw the early life experiences, violence, poverty, lack of love, lack of education, limited options, and foolish choices, and he found himself able to hold compassion for both the young girl and the perpetrator. In finding the root of suffering he saw the interconnectedness and realized that ending suffering requires compassion and help for both the victims and the perpetrators. He understood we are all the convict as much as the victim, we are all the dark as well as the light, "So, if you call me Thich Nhat Hanh, I will say, 'Yes, that is me.' And if you call me the young girl, I will say, 'Yes that is me.' If you call me the pirate, I will also say, 'Yes, that is me.' These are all my true names... All of these people are us. We inter-are with everyone"

When Meryl talks about her childhood experiences she is deeply sad. She has spent her life avoiding this part of herself, the small inner child who yearns for her love and attention. Early in her treatment she was closed down to this child completely, even feeling contempt for her. She felt her ugly and pathetic, unworthy of her compassion. When I would ask her what this part of her needed she had no idea. She'd been a wonderfully caring friend to so many people over the years, often the first one to help someone in need. She was a compassionate listener, and always had words of understanding and support. Yet when it came to what this neglected child inside her needed, she'd look at me blankly, shrugging her shoulders.

She had internalized so many of her early rejections and treated this part of herself as she had been treated by others—with impatience, dismissiveness, and rejection. But now, after working on self-soothing and emotional regulation, trust, communication of needs, and an acceptance of her flaws, she began to see this child through a very different filter. She could stand next to her now, instead of inside her, and offer her hand in loving kindness. This is the genesis of a reflective ego, the ability to stand outside one's pain with insight, understanding, and tolerance. Now we can truly begin the healing of the child.

Meryl asks me how can we help that part of herself,

who is in so much pain, now that we see and feel her? I enlist her beloved kittens to explore what true compassion feels like. "Remember a time when your cat was sick and afraid. Picture it in your mind," I instruct, "sense what it feels like in your body." Meryl reports feeling distressed, a sensation that feels heavy in her chest.

"How do you want to help her?" I ask.

"I want to hold her close to me," she says.

"So do that now," I say, "close your eyes and imagine how you would hold her. Perhaps pick up the pillow and position it how you would want to do so. Feel the energy you would be sending to her, like a bridge from your heart to hers, feel the transfer of that love and deep empathy and care."

Tears begin running down Meryl's cheeks. She nods her head in understanding. "Now send her healing energy Meryl, like prayers, send her your wish for her, to soothe her pain and calm her fear."

Her tears evolve into deeper sobs, as I sit silently near.

When she is finally spent, she slowly opens her eyes and looks at me with deep longing. The child inside aches terribly for what she never received and in giving her cat this kind of loving attention, she is overwhelmed by its absence in her own life.

"This is how we heal her," I say. "This is what you give her."

CHAPTER 16
Don't Believe Everything You Think

"He who fears he shall suffer, already suffers what he fears."
—*Michel de Montaigne, The Complete Essays*

Most people with OCD realize their rituals are irrational, however, some begin to believe they are effective in terms of their protection. Mom truly believed her rituals were keeping us all alive. She believed her constant washing kept illnesses away, that her relentless worrying kept accidents from happening, and her continuous checking kept the house standing.

A fear of the unknown is one of the greatest fears we face as humans. Uncertainty comes riddled with hypothetical what-if's and it is the job of the prefrontal cortex to enable us to be forward thinkers, giving us tools with which to plan and strategize our lives. The downside is that in planning we also have the ability to entertain a myriad of ways in which things can go wrong. Researchers reported in the journal Nature Communications that we have more than 6,000 thoughts per day. If we believe that all are real, accurate, and truthful we will wind up exhausting ourselves in attempting to control, change, and combat them. What an incredible waste of time and energy given to a pointless and random process. If, instead of believing our thoughts and using them as launching pads to rumination and worry, we defuse them instead, we may reserve our energy for the real issues in our lives, ones we can actually influence and control.

Helping clients to view the vast majority of their thoughts as random firings is helpful in increasing their ability to reason with internal dialogues. If I have a negative thought, let's say that as a parent I was so fatigued in raising a difficult child that I feared in actuality I regretted parenthood, and then unquestionably believed that thought to be real, I would naturally react with deep guilt and shame. But what if this thought is not real, but rather a feared thought. What if I only think I dislike parenthood because I love my child so much that I fear my anger is a sign of regret. When I stop and ask myself, "Is this thought 100 percent true?" I may see that it does not, in fact, speak to the entire picture. If something is only partially true then the follow-up question is "what else do I believe?" Well, I also believe that while my child makes me feel crazy at times there are other times when I would sacrifice my life for him. So then which is true, the former or the latter?

The answer is both. Sometimes I love parenthood and other times I long for a dry martini and a great book! This is dialectical thinking. When we refrain from seeing things through a split black and white, either/or filter and allow opposing facts and feelings to coexist we are able to have an integrative experience, one that is grounded in a more expansive perspective. Part of me is discontent and another part loving, another selfish and another compassionate. This is the complexity of our thoughts and feelings, they are not one thing or another. When we can make room for the contradictions we can attain greater equanimity and peace. It's okay to have horrible thoughts, just as it's okay to have wonderful ones. They all come and go and none define our value or our morality. An added bonus is that when we allow ourselves the negative thoughts they arise less frequently. I saw this often in couples therapy, once a spouse got the anger off their chest they no longer felt the words uttered to be true. They had held them back for so long, believing them without question, allowing them to fester and spin into stories, and when they finally hit the air they all felt like a lie. The look of shock and relief always struck me in those moments as though they'd been suddenly released of a toxin, so easily. If only they had communicated sooner.

We can do the same thing with catastrophic thoughts. Humans have no shortage of irrational fears and worst-case scenario thinking. We tend to focus on everything that can go wrong. There is an endless supply of what-if's and if we elect to follow them down the rabbit hole we are sure to meet a host of fascinating characters down there, most of whom are fictional, and unlikely to offer clarity or purpose. Why would any rational person choose such a path? We don't. It's reflexive, can you imagine actively trying to think

6,000 thoughts every day? And so we need to actively break out of the trance of mindless spinning. When we can pause to identify the thought, acknowledging it as random and insignificant, it disintegrates peacefully. It's as though we are saying to it, "I see you, now you can move along," to which it quickly complies in dissolving into a new awareness. We may have to repeat the process many times over, until the psyche finally lets up, but it surely will, we just need to keep practicing. As the bumper sticker says just "Don't believe everything you think."

The natural argument is what about the thoughts that are real and important. Certainly, I don't want to just dismiss everything as random firings of my brain. And certainly, we do not; but asking the question, "Is this thought a fact or 100 percent true?", allows us to filter down the amount of things that truly need our attention. If we don't, we may never have time to get to the important stuff, chasing our tails with nonsense in place of actual problem solving.

People who have OCD often suffer feelings of shame and guilt believing their thoughts to be real representations of who they are. Researchers Adam Radomsky and Jeff Szymanski conducted a study that showed while most of us have common intrusive thoughts, those with OCD have more negative reactions to them than those who do not. Also, the intrusive thoughts often represent those things that the person values most, like their loved ones or their religion. A thought, for example, of betraying one's family is not a true indication of the thinker's morality but is instead likely a response to family being of significant importance to them. We fear most hurting what we most love.   T h e reactions we have to our thoughts therefore are critically important, while the thoughts themselves are much less so. The act of resisting negative thoughts only fuels their frequency and intensity. Whenever we try to stop doing something, we do that very thing even more. It's quantum physics at work. That on which we focus increases and that which we resist persists.

When we look at adults who were raised in OCD households, intrusive thoughts are often central to their issues. Whether they inherited OCD or learned it environmentally is irrelevant. Their relationship to their thoughts must be explored and restructured. I often see these adults as parents now themselves, and there is a great fear in repeating the same mistakes as their OCD parent, hurting their children in ways they themselves have been hurt. They are worrying about their worrying and fighting their thoughts intensely, and losing the battle in the process.

The Buddhist practice of RAIN is a response protocol to managing our negative emotions. Whenever we notice them we have an opportunity to Recognize, Allow, Investigate, and Nurture. When we practice these steps we see just how quickly our feelings come and go. Neuroscientist Jill Bolte Taylor tells us the life cycle of any emotion is just ninety seconds! It is our reaction to the emotion that can last a lifetime.

The practice of RAIN helps us to observe thoughts rather than getting hijacked by them. Let's say we had a thought that a friend betrayed us in some way and that thought keeps arising and causing us to feel anger, resentment, and disappointment. We can stop and notice this by first Recognizing the feeling. It is helpful to name the emotion by saying, "Ah okay, I am feeling anger again. Here it is, I know this feeling. I can feel heat rising in my throat, tightness in my chest. My body feels braced for a fight." We then Allow this feeling by sending it "yes" energy versus "no" energy, allowing it to be just as it is rather than resisting and pushing it away. Like Rumi states in his poem, we open the door to whoever the visitor is, all are welcome. We can do this by expanding our lungs with a deep breath and slowly release it, visualize opening ourselves up to whatever occurs. We focus on making space for the feelings, to allow them to visit on their time, on their terms, just as they are. We can reassure ourselves in the process that we can tolerate them, that no one ever died from an uncomfortable emotion, and that we are okay. We can silently say yes to the feeling.

Sometimes Recognize and Allow is enough to satisfy the feeling and that is fine. Other times we may naturally progress into the Investigative stage. When we feel as though we have made peace with our emotions and they have subsided, we may then begin to Investigate by asking ourselves what these feelings are trying to teach us, or what they want us to know. We might explore what happened just prior to the feeling or what physical influences there might be such as illness or lack of sleep. In this way we cultivate a more curious mind, which serves as a great asset as curiosity will overshadow our potential self-judgments. We will also build a wise mind, gaining insight to our feelings as well as their triggers.

In the Nurture stage we send love and compassion to ourselves and the pain we are feeling. As we did with Meryl's kittens, we send healing energy to our struggle. We can place our hand over our heart as we do this, sending the vibration of loving awareness. We then allow ourselves to accept the nourishment freely and sit with it as long as feels right.

We may have to use the RAIN meditation a few times with the same emotion but we need to remember the goal is not to diminish our feelings or get rid of them in any way. It is to extend a bridge to them, honoring and respecting their roles in our lives and making peace with whatever arises.

Meditation has been a frequent practice for me for several decades, it is critical to my well-being. It is something I do without question or conscious intention, it's just part of my day. Other times, meditation is a tool I reach for in order to reset, generally when my ego is overly active and running the show.

One of the best ways to recalibrate is to attend a retreat. When we remove ourselves from our routine, and even our loved ones, we can focus in a more pure and uninfluenced way. We can gain insights and clarity that are so very difficult to attain in our normal environments. When I return from retreats I am better able to handle stressful relationships and react from a more balanced place.

The majority of my patients resist meditation because it requires being still with themselves and that is initially difficult for people who have traumatic wiring. They find the stillness threatening. Usually they approach meditation as a chore or exercise, with the goal of feeling better or changing in some way. They report doing it incorrectly because their minds won't stop thinking. But meditation is not about not thinking. Again, the more we attempt to stop doing something the more we are likely do it. It is the same with thoughts. The more we try to stop thoughts from arising the more thoughts we have. Instead, meditation is to be approached as an observation and redirection of thoughts. We watch as they arise, which they are certain to do, and then, instead of chasing the story of the thought, we gently nudge our focus back to our anchor, often the breath. We can do this a hundred times over again and, like push-ups for the brain, we build tolerance to uncomfortable thoughts and develop the ability to return to presence. Each time we achieve that redirection is a victory and with each victory we have made a positive change in our neural processing.

Why do we want a change in our neural networks? Because we are wired to react to our environment in a knee-jerk kind of response. As humans who desire mature and healthy relationships with each other and the world a slower response rate is more effective than the rapid response of animals to predators. When we have time to think through our reactions we can choose what is most appropriate. Viktor Frankl, a psychiatrist who survived the Nazi war camps and witnessed the murder of his entire family, helped other prisoners to create a reality for themselves in which they could survive psychologically. He said, "Between stimulus and response there is space. In that space is our power to choose our response. In our response lies our growth and our freedom." The practice of meditation helps us to create the space Frankl speaks of, the space necessary to live authentically free lives

CHAPTER 17
A Political Detour:
Managing Our Reactions

"No matter how much success you have, there will always be people who hate themselves so much that they'll gladly project that hate onto you." —Paul Ritchey

We live in an era of great anxiety due to the political divisiveness our leaders have created and the inauguration of fake news. What is happening in our country today is an enormous trigger for people who have been victim to the chronic manipulation of truth and reality. The "nothing to see here" defense denies our own ability to notice, reason, and conclude. We are, in essence, experiencing a national psychosis in that reality is distorted like a house of mirrors. It is why we take the fake news epidemic to heart. Our collective psyches understand the profound and psychological effects of denying one's truth, in that it offends our logical minds and thus our very humanity. The thing that separates us from animals is our ability to reason, it is the very basis of our evolution. It is also a critical road in maintaining our sanity. With a constant slow drip of misinformation and denials we are slowly losing our collective minds. It is how Hitler manipulated the Germans into the most unimaginable breakdown of their morality. If you successfully exploit a people's primal need for safety and convince them that they are in dire threat of the "other" they will raise their aggressive defenses instinctively.

A sizable percentage of our nation's populace will defend and extend former president Donald Trump's lies. I don't believe it to be malicious intent but like any cult-like brainwashing, there are those who are more vulnerable to following his lead. The threats he extols resonate with them, White America will soon be extinct. I recall in the late 70's a report predicting Caucasians would become the minority in America by 2050. I felt the panic around me at the time, living in what Bill Moyer's called in his documentary of my hometown, "A microcosm of racist America." Rosedale was the poster child of our national ills. In my neighborhood the homes of Black families were fire bombed. We received regular visits from white men letting us know in no uncertain terms that our fate would be similar if we sold to a Black family. Black children were harassed when riding their bikes past white kids playing in the street and the parents of my friends raised their middle fingers at Black men and women standing at bus stops. My hometown was ten miles down the road from Donald Trump's. Like mine, his neighborhood experienced an influx of diverse ethnic groups and a subsequent decline of what had been revered as a white safe haven. Our friends and families blamed the outsiders for the deterioration of our neighborhoods, which on the surface seemed true. In hindsight however, white people's anxiety wound up creating the very problems they feared. A 2003 report by PBS supports that it is who is moving out rather than who is moving in that triggers the decline of a neighborhood. Within a few years the violence in the neighborhood had become endemic.

Trump's inability, or more likely refusal, to work through his own fears has resulted in the mother of all projections. In a 2014 interview with Michael D'Antonio, he stated "I don't like to analyze myself because I might not like what I see." When we can't look at ourselves we instead cast a projection onto others, in his case "others" is the entire country and the country has become the canvas onto which his psyche splatters its poisons. The hateful vitriol has invited the darkness out into the light of day. While his base feels energized and freed by his attacks on political correctness, many fear we are losing our way in terms of truth and respect. We feel a weight upon our shoulders and are experiencing a collective depression and anxiety. *His* depression and anxiety to be clear. It has sprouted from his rejected and infantile self and from his self-hate we are in a hateful war against each other. Just as his siblings warred for the winning position in his family, we as a nation are dividing deeper. If we allow it, that is.

Over the past four years I have struggled with feelings of powerlessness and vulnerability. As the reports of immigrant children dying in cages came across my newsfeed

I felt sickened and terrified. Who would be the next "other" to be rounded up? A chill ran down my gay spine, as I know too well how that slippery slope ends. We do to one group what we are capable of doing to all. These are the nights I stay up strategizing my Canadian escape. We joke about it, but underneath there is a real fear of what we keep hearing over and over again—unprecedented times. A lack of history makes it feel that much more threatening, as though the worst is beyond our imaginations. Those notorious what-if's feed off the media incitements from either side, and everywhere we look we feel danger.

Trump needs to be stopped, I thought repeatedly, it all needs to stop! My fears compulsively sought a crumb of hope in anything that may rein him in. Certainly our government could do something to control him, our constitution, checks and balances, yada, yada, will save us. Yet over and over, his behavior would go unpunished, entangled in a political quagmire, and his tyranny started becoming the new normal. Like so many others I felt confused, disoriented. I no longer knew the country I had lived in for fifty-five years. I felt starved for validation of what I was seeing, hearing, and experiencing. Despite things being so incredibly blatant, I sought proof I was reading the cards correctly. I would watch the news, and even political comedy, for a sense of camaraderie in our communal appallment and angst. Is this really happening? Yes, yes it is, the TV said back.

The clock ticking on Trump's term offered no solace and I delved deeper and deeper into my despair until I hit the cruddy bottom of the psychic trash can. I needed to accept what was happening despite my fear and indignation or I was going to lose my own mind. In reality, it wasn't so much Trump who needed to stop, he was going to do what he does and will always do, it was me who needed to stop. My reactions were the only thing within my realm of influence and I worked on those the least. I needed to turn off the television, stop checking my news feed, and instead finally check in with myself. What was I needing and seeking below the surface of politics? What attention was my child-self wanting from me, the adult? When I stopped to listen, I heard her fear. She was terrified of someone stealing her truth again, terrified that I, the adult, would acquiesce to the manipulations and disown her reality, again. She was holding onto to her truth so tightly that I struggled to breathe. No one was going to deny her reality ever again, not even me. She was done with my mother's OCD, her denials of our experiences, my father's collusion, their looking the other way when threats abounded, and the normalizing of abnormal behavior. Trump was, to her, the figurehead of all her accumulated wounds and representative of every abuse she had ever known.

This is where the internal dialogue needs to begin. I am on her side, I am her protector, her advocate, her committed ally. I will never abandon her, never lie to or manipulate her, and never, ever allow anyone to take her own experience from her. From me she gets heard, and validation, and understanding. Her voice is real and it matters. She matters.

And finally, when she and I are talked out and exhausted, I put her to sleep in a safe, warm bed, with a gentle kiss on her forehead. Now and only now can we both rest.

Sometimes I practice the dialogue within a meditation. I begin by sitting somewhere safe and comfortable, closing my eyes and inviting the feelings to arise. It takes some reassurance sometimes to open up to the rawest of feelings and I need to take time in telling myself that it's okay to be uncomfortable, and that we will be all right. As the feelings begin to come up, I breathe into them, making more space in my chest, imagining a peaceful sea around them. They squirm and poke, jitters in my belly, burning in my chest, tightness in my neck, it's unpleasant. I breathe into the unpleasantness, sending love. Of course it hurts, I tell myself, it's scary and threatening and sad and mean and harmful and destructive and it feels frustrating and hostile and defensive and vulnerable. The more feelings I can name, the deeper I can go into them. I feel lost, confused, abandoned, hopeless, and then finally the tears come. I've had difficulty with crying, often needing to release tears, but unable to. Now they come freely and I sense they are old tears, a child's pain. As she processes I stand by her, protective and confident. I have her. In that moment I realize that my compulsion in watching the news cycles all day long has left her alone and scared, like my mother's neglect, I have been guilty of the same, of her, of myself. I get busy, like Mom, when I worry and I seek reassurance to appease the anxiety of uncertainty, when what I am needing, what she is needing, is to be here with it, together.

The next day I watch a single hour of news and I can feel the distance between me and it. It has lost its power over me and my feeling of anger is transformed into peace. I can meet the world where it is, how it is, what it is without a need to change or fix what is unfixable right now. I can watch it with the same opinions and same judgments but they no longer possess me. I have a clear sense of right and wrong and I know in my heart what is happening is an atrocity and I can still feel balanced, stable, centered, and clear. I can tailor my catastrophic spinning and while I may never be able to rein in the president I can rein in my reactions. When I heard the woes of my child-self, the adult stepped in to help balance her. I was able to see the numerous limitations of her vantage point. She could not see the forest for the trees and the trees were terrifying her. But with age comes experience and her adolescence beckoned my maturity.

Donald Trump has a role in our world, as major influencers often do. He is a masterful teacher for us to use, as he is a catalyst in waking up our unconscious darkness. He is a necessary evil in not only our nation's psychic development but for each of ours. He shines a light on our darkest repressions and brings forward our need to do more internal work. He has awakened our pain but in doing so has also awakened an opportunity for insight and healing.

The practice of internal dialogue helps us find the way. Sometimes we converse with our inner wisdom, the part of us that knows. We are taught and conditioned to seek answers outside ourselves but the real road map is unique and internal. Other people's maps don't apply to us and when we attempt to follow them we are dissatisfied with the destination. When, on the other hand, we ask our inner guides the questions we are amazed at how easily we hear the answers and how deeply they resonate with us. It feels right to us. If we have trouble hearing the messages we can tune into the body for help as it often knows before our thoughts do what is true and what is needed. When we are off our path we will feel tension, stress, and resistance in our bodies; we need only to pay attention.

When I was in college I had a friend I would meet for a weekly luncheon. Each time I would get a stomachache on the way there. I assumed it was another bout of IBS or my dairy intolerance despite the fact I hadn't indulged in anything suspect. I wish I had paid more attention to what it was trying to tell me because later in the term she wound up betraying me, cheating academically with my work. My inner guide knew long before it ever happened, knew this person wasn't someone I should trust. I didn't listen then but I do now. It was an invaluable lesson.

Dreams are also a wonderful guide for us and can bring our attention to where it's needed in our waking lives. Dialoguing with the characters in our dreams can be very helpful, asking them what they are wanting us to know. During meditation we can bring them up in our imagination and see what they have to teach us. We can also look for associations in our dreams, in what people, places, and things remind us of. Often the characters in our dreams represent parts of ourselves. It can be helpful to have dialogue between those parts. They may be in conflict or they may be able to offer help to each other.

There are so many creative ways we can process our difficult emotions and gain insight into them. There is no right or wrong way to practice. I had lost my childhood best friend in the World Trade Center on 9/11 and was in shock for quite sometime having watched the tower collapse into ashes on television. Some days later I went for a massage in Sedona, Arizona, a spiritual mecca to many. During the massage I dropped into a spacey kind of twilight state and I felt my friend Dolores hovering about. In my mind I heard her ask what I was doing. I told her the massage therapist was doing energy healing to which she flashed her familiar smirk, "Oh really," she said, "how much you paying for that?" She mocked affectionately. The conversation went on throughout the entire hour, as typical as any we had ever had. On some conscious level I knew I was creating the dialogue and yet on another level I felt she was speaking to me. I could not discern between the two afterward and I didn't feel a need to. It was my first experience with what Carl Jung called Active Imagination and I've used it as a way of exploring the entities within my psyche ever since. It can be a very powerful tool if you are willing to trust it.

CHAPTER 18
Secrets, Sex, and Other Skeletons

"Do not look for healing at the feet of those who broke you"
—Rupi Kaur, Milk and Honey

When I was a child I liked to wrestle with boys. Roughhousing was an outlet for me where I could expend my frenetic energy as well as challenge my place in the world. I didn't buy into the submission that came with my gender and enjoyed proving my power given any opportunity. I also had a difficult time staying still. I needed to be constantly moving. By today's diagnostic standards I likely would have been labeled ADHD. My second-grade teacher once put masking tape on my mouth to silence me and I frequently got called out for not paying attention. Schoolyard lunch breaks were my favorite time of day when I would run wildly, chasing and being chased. I was the girl who could beat the boys at their own games, often hitting harder and running faster. Never having actually seen me play, Dad would hear about my athletic proclivities and brag to his friends, prideful from a distance.

Regardless of the environment I could find a place and a circle of kids to run with, I brought my energy wherever my parents would take us. So it was in my parent's old Brooklyn neighborhood. One of my parent's friends there was especially fond of me and lit up when I showed up for their neighborhood stickball games. He rooted for me in Dad's felt absence, cheering me on as I sped past the makeshift bases, first the oak tree at Mrs. Russo's front curb, second the bumper of Mr. O'Leary's wood-paneled station wagon, and third Mrs. Gianotti's fence post, and finally the gritty manhole cover that was home base. He'd pat me hard on the butt as my teammates celebrated our victory.

Mr. Pappas knew me nearly my entire life, watching me evolve from diapers to diplomas. His attention was dramatic and animated and it made me feel special at a time in my life when that was lacking. But his larger than life persona made me uncomfortable, as did his overtly seductive ways. He liked the young girls and was unabashedly crude. Rumor had it that he "tried out" his son's girlfriends to ensure they were good enough. I didn't understand what that meant at twelve years old but I would come to learn.

He was masterfully entered my world through the things I loved most and playful wresting became our thing. He was strong like a bulldozer, both fat and hard. He'd pin me down, suffocating me with his weight until I would cry out uncle in surrender. I'd often wait until the last second as my stubborn pride wouldn't yield, until finally I'd eek out an "uncle" in a breathless gasp. With my face flushed bright red, I'd struggle to breathe air back into my lungs while he released a deeply satisfied laugh.

Sometimes we played while Mom had tea on the main floor of the brownstone with his wife. One particular day I went upstairs to join them post-concession. I sat at the table still breathless, trying to acclimate to their genteel, proper setting. I sat next to Mom, directly across from Mrs. Pappas who was staring at me with an odd smile. That's when Mom turned to look at me too, and noticed.

"What's that?" she asked, honestly bewildered.

"What's what?"

"On your neck? What's that mark on your neck?" she said in a raised octave.

Partly to escape their examination, and partly in confusion I ran into the bathroom to check the mirror. There I saw a bright purple, throbbing circle on the side of my neck. Mr. Pappas had taken the game to a new level that day. This time he hadn't heeded my cry of uncle but instead ground his pelvis into my unyielding groin. A new wrestling maneuver? I couldn't breathe and began kicking wildly for air, at which he pinned down my arms above my head, and buried his hot sweaty face into my dampened hair, grinding and grunting like an animal. Just as I thought I would lose all consciousness he released me and I fled to the stairs. I felt wild; feral, full of primal terror and adrenaline. I grasped the banister, eyes up toward at the old brown door separating house from basement, consciousness from repression. In my mind, I saw Mom's face, Mrs. Pappas' ambivalence, and paused my panicked flight as though in a dream, sinking in quicksand. Somewhere between the bottom step and the top my psyche had decided, I would be silent.

Staring at my reflection in the mirror I felt shame rising in my body. Why was the blood in my neck knotted like a bruise? Had he punched me? Certainly I would remember. I studied the circumference, stretching my skin between trembling fingers when it came back to me. It was that same mark I saw on my sister's neck when I was ten and had told Dad about in fear she had contracted some horrible disease. But instead of racing her to the doctor like I'd expected, he screamed at her while throwing her against the wall like a crash dummy. Clearly this purple moon was something bad and now it was on me like a scarlet letter. What could I say to defend my ignorance, or innocence? It didn't seem like anything would point the blame away from me to where it rightly belonged. Adults always won in my world and children always got sacrificed. There was no reason to hope for anything more here. So I returned to the kitchen, to my seat at the table and faced their scrutiny.

"I don't know," I said, "Mr. Pappas did that to my neck." I watched as the two women traded glances, one more expressionless than the other. Mrs. Pappas was the first to weigh in, "Well that's my husband, he likes to play," she said vacantly. I held my head down in silence, awaiting Mom's assessment. Maybe she would be on my side after all, she had always warned me about boys who would try to go too far. She was disgusted with men and sex and found it all loathsome. She cringed at my sisters "love bite," certainly she'd be upset with Mr. Pappas for doing this to her youngest daughter. But the silence sat and sat until I couldn't bear its weight. I looked up at Mom for a response, searching for her defense, but her head was down, like my own had been, bent low in shame. "Mom?" I beckoned. She shrugged her shoulders as if to say, "What are you gonna do?", and that was the end of it.

Six years later when I told Mom that "Uncle Ernie" (a pseudonym I'd adopted from the rock opera *Tommy for my actual uncle*) who had lived upstairs from us, was a child molester, she gave me that same silent reaction and shrug of surrender. She appeared just as indifferent as that day at the Pappas' house. There was no waking her up, nothing I could do or say or scream that would provoke a reaction in her. I tried for years to ignite any response at all, but nothing broke through her icy glare. The harm done at this point to me and our relationship was beyond anything we had faced prior and I promised myself I would never forgive her.

And I never have. A couple of years ago the topic came up again, as do most of Mom's conflicts, disguised innocently inside the minutia. I told her it still upset me that she never said anything at Mrs. Pappas' table that day, and as far as I knew, never said anything to anyone, including me. "Well," she said defensively, "I didn't want to upset her or have her upset with me. She's been a very good friend to me, she always included me, she was good like that," and then with a slight chuckle she continued, "you know, she called me a peculiar bird once, because I never asked for help. Rather die I would. I guess I'm just funny that way." And once again, that was the end of it. Forgiveness never had a chance.

Mom is a colluder. She rubbernecks away from the crash. Even if she didn't know about Uncle Ernie, once she learned the truth she refused to integrate the new data, like a broken processor. After I moved out I had come to visit one Sunday afternoon. My aunt and her vile husband were in the kitchen with Mom and Dad. As I walked into the room and saw them all there, I knew I'd have to make a quick calculation of risks in self-preservation. The thought of planting my lips on one on my uncle's stubbly, greasy cheeks made my stomach lurch. But if I skipped over him it would be noticed and Mom had hijacked me into her secrecy. No one was to know about his child-sex proclivities, not even his wife, most especially not his wife. Mom said her sister wasn't mentally well and would have a break down if she knew the truth. She had had them before, receiving shock treatment years prior when their mother had died. So our job was to protect her, even if it meant we were to protect a perpetrator.

Even Dad was kept out of the knowing. I was conflicted about whether or not my fantasy of him slaying the demon would be as satisfying in reality since he'd likely wind up in prison. Mom had once given me the option by saying, "If you really hate me and want to see me suffer you will tell your father." Well, in that moment I did hate her and want to see her suffer but I still didn't tell my father. I didn't feel it was my place as I wasn't the one he abused and it wasn't my story to tell.

Standing now in the kitchen, thick in my quandary, I quickly deduced the best approach was to not greet anyone in the room with the obligatory kiss so as not to call attention to the one kiss I'd omit. As I stood at a distance in the doorway I waved a collective hello as eight eyes stared at me in waiting. "Hi," I offered, as they stayed silent. I scanned the room hoping for them all to just go about their business but we were stuck in an awkward standstill. I couldn't help but glance at the uncle, who was a large, overweight man subscribed to the old school of personal hygiene—that is, weekly baths. Clearly he required more frequent upkeep as he emitted what could only be described as a toxic mist. I shuddered.

Mom came toward me smiling, "Don't you say hello to your mother?" asking playfully. I kissed her cheek on command and knew I was doomed. I began then to make the rounds, kissing my aunt but instead of then making my way to the uncle I scooted behind him to kiss my father. The tension in the room was undeniable. At the obvious completion of my rounds Mom started at me, "Juliane, kiss your uncle!" I stood frozen between the two men, wishing like a child that one would smite the other in my honor. My legs shook beneath me as Mom was now scolding and Dad's posture grew stiff like the tail of a dog ready to attack. I knew what was happening, that this whole charade was meant to preserve my aunt's dignity and honor, while incinerating mine to ashes as an unfortunate but acceptable casualty. I was the sacrifice at the altar of denial and although Mom had claimed to give me the last life vest on the boat when I asked her as a child who she would save, my aunt or me, I never doubted it would be me who'd wind up at the bottom of the sea. Once again I had to choose between safety and violence and once again my fear overruled my self-respect. I kissed that horrid man as instructed and at twenty-two years old, doubted I would ever be free of my family's oppression.

Mom lives in two worlds, one is her fairy-tale fantasy of princes on white horses who show up at the last moment to save the fair maidens, and the other a reality in which sex is filth. In her fantasy, women were revered without having to pay the price of fornication. For this reason, she will only watch PG-rated movies, because they depict love without sex. It isn't completely surprising considering her generational upbringing but the contradictions were confusing to me growing up. She declared sex a chore, something you had to do for your husband. By twelve years of age I had believed that sex and enjoyment either didn't coexist or was a perversion of sorts. I joked with my friends that Mom and Dad each kept their rubbers in their respective nightstands, Dad's Trojan and Mom's Playtex. But there was nothing funny about my confusion, and as though it wasn't difficult enough to deal with my sexuality and the guilt and shame that came with it, Mom's frigidity and Dad's hypersexuality were head spinning. As were the contradictions. Mr. Pappas and Uncle Ernie were granted mind-bending absolutions and as abhorrent as sex was to Mom, it was our setting off the alarm that was the problem, not the assault or the assailant. We were not afforded righteous anger in response, since in her mind, as women and as children, we hadn't any agency.

My experience in Mr. Pappas' basement left me with an angry wound so deep I wanted to scream it out at times. But instead of directing it at him, it always aimed right at Mom's betrayal. It simply hurt more. But Mom was never going to change course on her reaction and she would never help me to move on from it, so there I was stuck, for years. Right in that same place.

Sometimes we can't invoke the help of those who have harmed us in the healing process. Some are now deceased, some are too unsafe, and some are like Mom who are incapable of reflection. So we have to get creative in doing it without them. I have written many letters, addressed to various people who have hurt me over the years. It is a very freeing exercise in which you allow yourself the expression of your rawest thoughts and feelings without filters or repercussions. The letters aren't meant to communicate to the receivers but to process our pain without them. Sometimes we burn them in a symbolic gesture of alchemizing them to ashes. I have had some clients send them up in balloons, some buried them in the ground; there are all kinds of creative ways to help our psyches let go of their wounds.

The things we write might surprise us, thinking ourselves incapable of such horrible thoughts or feelings.

But it's a cathartic release of the accumulated residue we've been storing. We have learned to bypass our wounds, remove them from our day-to-day awareness, and despite their silence they act as heavy weights that can cause us to lose vitality in our lives, leaving us feeling depressed and joyless.

Some say we should forgive others because in doing so we can let go of negative feelings. But I think the letting go process is too complicated to meme. First we need to really feel our anger. Buddhists are not proponents of giving our negative emotions expression, instead they use loving awareness to defuse them. But in my own experience we first need to give a voice to the oppressed being inside us. We live in the physical world after all and most of us do not spend hours each day in meditation. We therefore need to synthesize our experiences in a more approachable way. The process letter is very effective in giving negative feelings a form with which we can work directly. Otherwise they are ghosts roaming freely. Once we give our wounds expression we often feel relieved of their toxins, and a sense of calmness takes over. Other times we need to write a series of letters as we may have more to say. The relief we feel may be immediate, gradual, intermittent, or come in stages.

Sometimes when the offense is so great that it resists our work in letting go, we can then use another form of the exercise. Interestingly, our brains don't recognize the difference between what is real and what is imagined in terms of healing. If you want to test the brain's incredible power just look at the reports of people using hypnotherapy in place of anesthesia during surgery. Without any medicinal intervention the brain is able to block pain to the point of allowing the body to be cut open with a scalpel. It's impossible to exhaust the potential of what our minds can do. Utilizing this advantage we can write letters from those who have harmed us, giving them the voice we choose, writing the words we need to hear, and choreographing our wished-for acknowledgment and apologies. My patients often respond with a skeptically raised eyebrow at this suggestion yet admit to feeling lighter after they've done it. One patient reported passing her nemesis in the hallway at work the next day and being surprised at her lack of reaction, "It was as though she were any other coworker. I even gave her the mindless head nod as I passed her by. She was nobody special anymore." This articulates the experience beautifully. We are unintentionally assigning our enemies a special designation, hardly something we would consciously choose. By processing our anger we pull back our projections and instead of holding leading roles our abusers become the inconsequential extras in our storylines.

Chapter 19
The Cycles of Love and Hate

"There comes a time in your life when you have to choose to turn the page, write another book or simply close it."
—*Shannon L. Alder*

Forgiveness can be a long process, with lots of twists and turns. Having to keep Uncle Ernie's secret caused an already tenuous relationship with Mom to be even more fractured. I experienced what felt like the ultimate abandonment, something I would never be able to move past. All of her OCD'ing had by this point resulted in a cavernous gap between us, it had broken down my trust and landed our bond in the dustbin. I felt lower in her priorities than ever before and a burden she was forced to endure. And now I represented a threat to her, a keeper of minacious secrets, and if I attempted to talk to her about any of it she looked at me as though I was the perpetrator. The uncle didn't know we knew, my father was still in the dark, my brother kept his head in the sand, my aunt (the wife) was spared a single moment of angst in having married a pedophile, and my sister and I carried the family's sludge like sherpas of shit.

Still, we managed the illusion of family, like divorced parents speaking only as needed. We managed, we believed, to fool outsiders with our feigning of a cohesive family, perhaps with the usual flaws but certainly no ominous skeletons to be found in our closets. Our disease hid from sight like a silent cancer hides from not only its host but everyone in its orbit. The untrained eye is blind to its incubation, and as it metastasizes behind your back, it's game over before you ever realize it was there.

Our endings were many, as Mom and I piled up wound upon wound, each feeling like the ultimate and last, each building yet another layer of scar tissue around my heart. It all came to a head for me on Mother's Day when I was about twenty years old, a day that no longer held any importance to me but was rather a dull reminder of our nonexistent relationship. Unfortunately for me, Dad wasn't privy to the how's and why's of my disengagement and his understanding of me defaulted to an assumption of immature selfishness and disrespect. Of course he would expect me to join them for dinner, why wouldn't he?

My plans, however, didn't include Mom but instead a visit to a friend who lived in the city, who was grieving the loss of her own mother. We had grown close and she felt like my real family. I was intent on going. But I would need an escape plan which I hadn't formulated.

As I passed the living room on my way to the front door I caught Dad's glare in my peripheral vision, and all hope for invisibility was gone.

"Where are you going?" he asked indignantly, peering over his readers.

"To meet Nicole," I mumble. He popped out of his seat as though ejected by force.

"It's Mother's Day!" he informs me, inches from my face.

"Yes, I know that," I assured him. "I promised I would spend the day with Nicole, she's really upset her Mom died last month. I need to go." I am no more convinced by my tone than my enraged father. I know fully that it's a lame attempt, how can he possibly understand?

"Oh, you think so do you? You are most definitely not going. You have your own mother, who is very much ALIVE and you will have dinner with us."

"I can't cancel now, she's expecting me," I say flatly.

The veins in my father's head are bulging blue striations and his eyes are searing in anticipation. Outrage is a drug for him, one he abhors and adores equally and simultaneously. He is righteous in his mind, fighting the fight against whatever injustice he perceives. Today it's in the name of his wife's honor despite the fact that neither she nor I believe this for a moment. Dad's rage is all about him, and a legacy of violence that has been passed down generationally, a poisoning of DNA. He'd threaten beatings at the slightest infractions, at crying babies, children acting out at the mall, even characters on TV, "If that were my son I'd take him by the throat and slam his head through the door." It was his fantasy to harm, destroy, annihilate any challenge to his authority, real or perceived, as though it would somehow affirm his strength and valor. The only thing that stood in the way between fantasy and reality was Mom. She'd intercept as the damage befell us, and only just prior to catastrophe, but not before my incredibly busy brain would prepare its demise, flooding my nervous system with chemicals that would forever linger. Dad knew how to make us chronically fearful, like a trained terrorist. He had learned from his father how to pump up the anticipation to the point that it didn't matter if he hit you or not. Your central nervous system was fooled just the same.

He would yank the leather belt off his jeans, cutting it though the air like a whip past my face. That chilling crack at the tail end conditioned me like a lab rat. I experienced his wrath at a dizzying speed, and each time I would think, this is it. Today he will surely kill me, kill us all. This time Mom would be too late and find our dead bodies strewn on the floor. And maybe, just maybe, we'd all be better off. I had begun to fantasize about revenge with my own demise. Maybe if he killed me then finally he'd pay. It would be my only shot at justice because certainly no one was coming to save us and it was getting harder for Mom to hold him back. Sometimes he'd stop but other times he threw her out of his path. You just never knew. But as terrified as I was of the physical violence there was nothing worse than being the object of my father's hate. That was the real violation. It assaulted a place in me that was deep and primal, the part of me that knew a child was entitled to a parent's love and protection. It insulted that truth at an archetypal level and I knew in my bones that my reality was profoundly and collectively wrong.

On this day, however, there wasn't time for any terrorist foreplay and Dad got straight to the point.

"You are not leaving this house. Do you hear me my darling daughter?" He has me by the hair now and is pulling me toward the wall.

"I am," I whispered, breaking the camel's back.

He grabbed the chain that held my grandmother's cross around my neck. The grandmother who had been canonized in her death before I was born. Mom had passed it on to me, entrusting me with its safety. I never took it off.

"And you wear this like it means something," he contorted. "You selfish, spoiled bitch. You don't give a damn about family."

He spewed the words in my face all the while twisting the chain into my neck and while I didn't feel pain I suspected it should hurt. His caustic words buzzed around my head unintelligibly, like a record on a too-slow speed, wobbling and alien. In my memory, I recall my head banging against the wall in an obscene rhythm,

"You" bang, "will" bang, "be" bang, "with" bang, "your" bang, "mother" bang, "tonight" bang, with an emphasis on YOUR.

I recall the sensation of whiplash. Maybe he wasn't hitting me against the wall, but shaking me back and forth, or maybe it was just his words shaking me from the inside out. It's impossible to report as it's happening, there's more data coming in than my mind can process. But his message breaks through like rumbling thunder before the flash, he's grunting his final warning at me, to do with it as I will, daring me to defy him. There is a small voice inside that begs me to stand down, as only my compliance will calm the beast, but I cannot submit. Not this time. I want only to contest, to refuse being broken, if only my lungs would reinflate and give a voice to my rebellion. All I manage is a winded shake of my head, a lifeless "no." It is a pathetic attempt to raise a rubber sword, and yet it manages to re-stoke his rage as though I'm a true warrior. The final bell has clanged in his head and he comes at me showing the world that he and only he is the reigning champion, and no contender will survive his terror.

Here enters Mom. In a split moment she assesses the danger, it is instinctual by now, its energy obvious. She is screaming as she runs toward us, demanding my father let me go, which he does with a shove rather than a release. "What are you doing Vinny? What happened this time?" she scolds.

My father relays my intention for the evening to her like a pouting child. "Well, if she wants to go, let her go. I don't want her there anyway," she says, exposing again her topsy-turvy indifference. While she cares very much that I not be killed by my father in her foyer, she cares not at all whether or not I am at her Mother's Day dinner. They exchange glances of agreement. I am beyond hope, a miserable failure despite their best efforts, and a waste of their genetic potential. "Good," he spits in my face, "your friend can have you."

The hand-off is complete. I have set the table knowing that I can honor my boundaries and protect myself from aggression and oppression but I will in the future have to eat alone, and so be it.

A stranger looking through our window would have gotten the story all wrong. They would have mistakenly assumed Mom the good guy and Dad the bad, Mom the savior, Dad the villain. But Mom was every bit as angry as Dad, perhaps angrier, only her OCD locked her anger behind a heavily guarded gate. She needed Dad, who did not have a lock on his gate at all and would fling it open wildly at the slightest provocation. She says she didn't want him to hit us, but to talk to us, to control us, but beneath the surface I suspect she wanted to throw that shoe that had missed my brother's head as much as my father wanted to throw his fist. But her guilt denied her rage and his was a proxy that worked for them both.

Therapists refer to this as doing each other's unconscious work. In Family Systems Therapy we attempt to identify the feelings and behaviors that are repressed and the ways in which other members within the family may be acting them out in an unconscious attempt at homeostasis. The easiest one to see is the anger tradeoff. Imagine you had a horrible day at work, and your boss really got under your skin. You go home and begin to complain about it when barely a paragraph in, your spouse goes off the rails in your defense, likening your boss to the dictator he is. If repression is a variable you might no longer feel angry as your spouse's tirade blares on in the distance, but instead tire of the whole thing.

Whereas before you wanted to scream yourself, now you'd rather just go take a bath. You've never been good at expressing your anger anyway and your judgment of temper tantrums is pretty poor. Your spouse on the other hand seems not to mind lashing out and in fact even seems to enjoy his raging indignations. In essence, you and your spouse have an unconscious contract in anger expression and management. This creates problems for both parties as you may never work through your angry feelings and your spouse will thus be labeled the angry one.

Notice, I said that this will happen if repression is a variable. When our anger is not repressed or conflicted we often don't feel better when others do our work for us but rather stifled and shut down. It doesn't feel good to have the bone taken away from us when we need to chew on it awhile. It's a process that metabolizes negative feelings, to be able to talk them through, unknot the psyche, and hear ourselves advocate for things we believe in and value. It is in this way that we can see ourselves from a distance, and partner up in the healing.

Interestingly, when we begin to do own anger work and allow ourselves to express our feelings, our "angry" spouses often begin to feel less so and surprisingly more tolerant.

This is because they are no longer carrying our anger on top of their own. Suddenly, personalities don't seem quite as fixed but rather more fluid. As I change, you change, and hence we change as a family.

In my home Dad took the anger baton from Mom and was off to the races. She in turn got to play the role of protective mother as she pulled him off me. She was the peacekeeper, the mamma bear, when more often than not we all fought because of her. Dad had gained the reputation Mom had wanted for him on an unconscious level. She married him, knowing beneath the denials that he would fulfill the role she needed him to play; he was actually perfect for the part. And as stealthy the strategy, I always knew Mom had puppeteered his bad behavior just as she had mine so many times.

One night, still young at about age eleven, I woke up to find my father sitting on the floor of my bedroom, in the dark, sobbing. I don't remember what he had done but it was typical for him to be remorseful after a Mom-driven event. He was apologizing and pleading forgiveness in a raw moment of vulnerability. He admitted to hating himself, and wanting to be a better man than his father. I had already forgiven him. He was my world. As hated and hateful as I felt, I still loved him. It's the dialectical once again, a mixture of complex and contradictory feelings happening together. Later, Mom asked what he had said to me. I could see she was wanting to control my feelings. She warned that Dad manipulates people into trusting him again, and that I should learn from her mistakes. Her words poured cold water on my softening heart, and my feelings of compassion were quickly overshadowed by anger, but not for my father as she had hoped. It was she I felt I could never trust, because she was incapable of tearful apologies or any self-reflection and we could never have moments like the ones I had with Dad.

In counseling we speak to the repairs in relationships. As I mentioned earlier humans have a great capacity for adversity and their propensity toward psychological recovery is great. Marriage expert Dr. John Gottman explains the need for couples to get beyond their most heated conflicts with an effort at repairing the damage afterward. He believes that relationships can weather the harshest storms with the right repair. We can make these repairs in a number of ways but most are effective when they are from a place of accountability and vulnerability. When we take full ownership of our behavior and seek to truly understand the other person we are generally good at making them. Sometimes it's a heart-felt apology, sometimes it in an acknowledgment of the other person's experiences, but all are intended to breach the gap of conflict.

My father made a wonderful repair that night in my bedroom. I would love to report that it made a difference in our relationship but it didn't. As my mother warned, Dad's apologies and repetition of the same behaviors were, in fact, his pattern. I don't believe them to have been malicious manipulations but rather failed attempts at change. He attempted change through resolutions. As in his early marriage promise to never hit my mother again, and his pledge to my mother to never hit us kids with a closed fist. These concrete, measurable standards that he set for himself were indeed attainable for him, but he lacked the will and skill for self-reflection and analysis. He had been through too much in his life to fully fix the cracks in his foundation. They ran too deep and he simply didn't think the why of his behavior mattered—he looked forward not back.

So like the dry alcoholic he wasn't actively using but his "-ism" remained. While the violence ratcheted down over the decades, especially once we all made it out of the house, he still ran on his grandiose ego. His narcissistic world view drove him and so in his world there is no other, he saw no one else's emotional, psychological and spiritual needs. We were all solely projections of his narcissistic grandiosity. We were all possessions, not individuals, in his regime. So while the physical attacks petered out, the anger remained his constant companion. And we all saw the companion there, an oil slick on the surface waiting for ignition, and so we never fully relaxed in his presence. It didn't stop me from loving him but it did stop me from trying to change him or have a relationship of any greater substance with him.

CHAPTER 20
The Second Arrow

"Suffering is pain multiplied by resistance"
—*Buddha (attributed)*

When I was a child I was forbidden to communicate my upset in any way, even facially. After Dad raged at me, I wasn't to show my fear and anger. If my eyes betrayed me and showed any sign of distress he would start berating me again. Controlling my facial muscles became a survival skill that helped me avoid more punishment, but would unfortunately complicate my relationships later in life. It is difficult for others to feel safe and loved when I freeze, and it's a process I've had to work through for years. It became critical for those closest to me to know this part of my story, and to understand that while I may look like I am unfeeling, I am actually over-feeling. I have been fortunate to have had partners who were willing to do the work with me. But it required an enormous amount of communication and vulnerability to get through the layers.

Many of my patients grew up in homes where their emotions were either shut down or shamed. They learned to do the same to themselves as adults, repressing their feelings or feeling embarrassed by them. We learn quickly as children to morph ourselves into what the parent wants or needs, and if our negative emotions cause them distress we may begin to dissociate from our feelings. As adults we may wonder if something is wrong with us for lacking certain emotions. What is rejected and denied as children often gets disowned in a kind of splitting off. When we place our thoughts, feelings, traits, etc. into categories of good versus bad, positive versus negative, we attempt to be one over the other rather than accept all as human inevitabilities. That process of splitting causes us to repress parts of who we are, which then get projected onto others. When we can accept our flaws compassionately we are better able to work on them, improving ourselves and developing an integrated personality, full of the myriad qualities in their genuine forms. It is a beautiful process when we are curious about the things we don't like about ourselves, when we can pause and notice, "Wow that was interesting, I just got really irritated there without even realizing it. I wonder what that was about?"

In my own experience, I had to keep my anger at a distance in order to protect myself. I only expressed it when my father wasn't home. My mother took the brunt of the rage I felt for my father, as I thought her a safe place to vent. In reality it was not safe at all, since my projected anger wound up coming back full circle. There was one time when I took my anger out on Mom about having to deal with accounting classes that I hated and that made me feel incompetent. I was angry at my father for making me choose a subject I hated as a major but I could never express that anger at my father, the consequences too severe. So instead I yelled at my mother about my father, and fired some insults directly at her for good measure. She did little to argue back and my only clue of her disapproval was the pressing of her lips tighter and tighter until they nearly disappeared altogether, but later she called him at work and blasted a litany of complaints at him about how nasty I was. My father was barely through the front door when he threw his briefcase at the sofa and charged at me fists and jaw clenched.

"You think you can speak to your mother like that," he barked, "like the animal that you are?" As he threw his hand back to slap me my mother pulled back his arm, crying her usual, "Don't hit her, I just want you to talk to her."

"You can't talk to them," he yelled back, "you have to beat sense into them or they don't listen."

I may as well have expressed my anger directly at my father for all the good it did me to go through the back door, at least I would have felt like I had a voice and was able to stand up for myself. I still have to remind myself not to keep using that route when I'm upset today, because it amounts to passive-aggressiveness and what we call triangulation, using a third party to communicate our issues instead of directing our anger at the source.

Consequently, the work I needed to do on my anger was delayed from spending so much time on the projection merry-go-round and I would wait years before I could safely express my feelings. In my early relationships my anger came out like a steam valve released—too much, too hot not to burn. Once I gave it permission I couldn't stop it, and shame and self-loathing were quick to follow. I hadn't yet learned that to express anger effectively I had to first truly make peace with it. Allowing myself to express anger while still believing that I was bad or wrong for feeling it transformed it into rage instead of the cathartic release I needed. It took time to accept the idea that anger isn't the enemy and in fact is a necessary emotion. It drives us into positive action when used properly. If we don't feel the burn of the hot iron we won't understand its danger in the same way, and similarly, anger tells us that something needs our attention. We take it seriously when we feel the discomfort of the emotion.

A patient of mine lived in an unhappy and oppressive marriage for years, never acknowledging her anger. Had she known just how angry she was she could have fought and advocated for herself instead of being mindlessly led into submission. But since her feelings had been deemed excessive and unjustified as a child she began to dissociate from them and in not knowing her feelings she failed to do what she needed to do.

When we look at our emotions as catalysts to positive change we can partner instead of war with them. When we are anxious we can explore what it is we are avoiding, as anxiety is an effective motivator to changing our lives and overcoming complacency. Without it we would likely not progress as a species but become stagnant. But as soon as we feel anxious we assume something is wrong with us. We seek calm, having a bath or a drink or a pill. There's nothing wrong with seeking relaxation, however, if we do so in substitution of exploration and reflection we build more avoidance, and thereby more anxiety.

I am often asked how to process our emotions. We talk a lot about the concepts of unpacking our conflicts and working through our feelings but how exactly do we do that? One of the greatest of tools for me is the written word. I discovered early in life that writing about my experiences and emotions was cathartic, and held a space for me to deposit what I couldn't digest. Putting words down on paper satiated my need for an organized mind, and a coalescence of my experiences. Whenever I felt overwhelmed I'd journal by identifying and describing what was happening in my life, just like the RAIN meditation suggests. At the time I didn't realize I was doing a mindfulness practice, I saw it as a way of maintaining my truth. The psyche pushes us toward this process, to reflect and make sense of our lives. I have found that the most distressed patients I have encountered are those without narratives. They are not able to tell their stories in a way that is cohesive or that provides meaning in their pain. When we can see where the twists and turns have led us and realize the degree of learning and growth that resulted from them, we can better accept the painful past and its value in our journey. We can make peace with it. But instead, if we feel like our lives are a random hodgepodge of pain and trauma without any insight or meaning, then we might view life as a brutal reality filled with fruitless suffering, or as my mom used to say, "If life is a bowl of cherries then what I am doing in the pits?" We also have an opportunity to rewrite the story we tell ourselves when we look at the facts and realize that our perceptions have tainted our realities.

While my journal may have seemed filled with nothing more than random teenage angst, it held between its covers, my story. And in storing my experiences, they held for me what I could not. My journals were in essence the containers for my heart and my psyche. The pain I felt as a child was expansive and beyond my comprehension but writing words on paper was like handing my emotions over to a divine mother who would keep them safe for me.

In documenting my experiences I was also able to keep conscious. My sister is always surprised by how much I remember and how I have been able to put the story together. I think it was the many hours of writing that kept my psyche from jumping into the abyss. Without consciousness I would have likely fallen into the denials much of my family had and while being aware is tremendously painful, it is the core of our healing.

So although I was late to the processing party I had a strong basis from which to build. My story and narrative provided a better understanding of what I needed. Dad had shut down my experiences but I managed to find a place to be heard and validated. Where I wasn't permitted to be angry and cry and throw things at the wall, I could write and no one could take that away from me.

Writing isn't for everyone and it's not the only way we get to process our pain. The practice of RAIN is our standby whenever difficult emotions arise. Taking a pause in itself is often helpful. Simply stopping to notice and observe the present moment changes the neural firings in our brains, giving us a window of opportunity to consider the facts of a situation. Sitting in stillness and watching the constant changes in our experience reminds us that thoughts and feelings are fleeting. A favorite meditation of mine is one in which you observe your experiences. In the first part you notice your thoughts, and identify them as either planning or remembering, or you simply state 'thinking' as the thoughts arise. In the moment of naming the thought it vanishes almost immediately and another follows, to which you repeat the process. After several minutes the thoughts begin to slow down, the gaps between them getting longer. Those spaces in between are so grounding and I often experience a centering sensation in the stillness of the mind. In the next part of the meditation we observe changing sensation. I have followed an itch to its passing which I never thought possible! It's hard to believe no one has ever died from not scratching yet there you have it. Tracking the intense burning and craving to relieve the itch is a learning experience in itself. The lesson being that everything we experience, be it discomfort or pleasure, passes and in the reality of impermanence comes freedom from stuck-ness. The neuroanatomist Dr. Jill Bolte Taylor tells us that any given emotion has a lifespan of ninety seconds. That's hard to believe, especially during the last four years of constant turmoil and the seemingly longest year in history, 2020.

The ninety-second lifespan, however, does not include our reaction to the emotion. Think of the last time you banged your toe into a table and the immediate emotion that came up and how quickly it went away. Seemingly it arose with the pain and left with it as well. This is because we didn't spin a story about stubbing our toe, we stubbed it, it hurt, it stopped hurting, and we moved on. Imagine if we berated ourselves about stubbing our toe and told ourselves how stupid and clumsy we were or blamed whoever moved the table causing me to stub my toe. I could go on for hours in this way all the while feeling the negative emotions, a lot longer than ninety seconds. The Buddhists call this concept the second arrow, the arrow of suffering. The first arrow is the pain that precedes the suffering, the stubbing of the toe. Pain is inevitable and a necessary reality. Suffering is not. While pain is short-lived, suffering can last a lifetime. When we choose not to create stories about our pain we can limit our difficult emotions to the ninety seconds as the research shows.

Lastly, another favorite way to process feelings is to get out in nature, and I mean really get out, as in take off your shoes and socks and walk upon the earth. We are so oblivious in our culture to the healing properties of the life around us. Allow the subtle movement of trees to linger in your awareness, nourish your senses in the experience of the wind, of water, of light and dark, of the sounds around you. Focus on each step as your foot touches the ground, as though caressing it with your toes. Walking mediation in nature is a home run for emotional resetting in my book. Try it!

CHAPTER 21
No Good Deed...

*"There can be no deep disappointment where
there is not deep love." —Martin Luther King, Jr.*

When I was an intern at a nonprofit clinic I worked with an indigenous population who were living on the fringe. We offered programs to assist with basic living requirements such as food donations, clothes, diapers, etc. We saw the poorest of the poor and some of the cruelest heartaches I could have imagined. One client in particular, a middle-aged Native American man who lived on the reservation and had a brutally traumatic history, really pulled at my heart when, after working so hard to keep his sobriety and maintain an income, had his bicycle, his only means of getting to work ten miles away in the Arizona desert, stolen.

I remembered seeing some bikes in the donation room so I excitedly wrote up a request substantiating his need. My supervisor, after receiving my request called me in to her office wanting to know why I was wanting the bike for my client. Hadn't she read my plea? I gave her his story, with genuine

251

emotion, confident that she would share in my heartache.

"But why do you want to give him a bike?" she asked. Clearly, she still wasn't getting it.

"So that he can get to work and keep his job," I said.

"Yes, I understand, but why do *you* want to give him a bike?" she repeated with emphasis.

Clearly I wasn't getting it. She turned down my request and I was indignant the rest of the day, feeling superior in my compassion and morality.

When I saw my client that week he entered my office beaming. He had traded some car maintenance work with another man on the reservation for an old jalopy of a bicycle. His eyes flashed self-satisfaction in a way I will never forget. How would he have felt instead had I came in that day, beaming with my own self-satisfaction, playing the savior in his sad melodrama? That's what my supervisor was trying to tell me. Why did I want to get him a bike? So that I could be the hero rescuing the poor and needy. Problem being, of course, was that my client didn't need saving, he needed to be his own hero and he was.

I realize it sounds like an argument against welfare, however, there are plenty of times when that donation room is used, and used wisely. There is an important difference between enabling, rescuing, and legitimate aid. As therapists we need to know when to step back and when to step in. It's a close call sometimes, but if we are truly honest with ourselves and our egos we usually know what we need to do.

Prior to my client teaching me about boundaries, I felt a relentless need to save people from their pain, not even pain, their very discomfort. As though in some unknown way I had created it and therefore must now resolve it. I have felt the burden of needing to know the solutions and if I didn't have them, then to find them. It's hard to reckon whether or not I put this on myself or it was dropped on my shoulders from a higher source—Mom. I knew that the most important thing in the world was not to cause Mom stress of any kind. This included getting sick. We were never to become ill because Mom wouldn't be able to handle it, which is a strange kind of pressure. As it is we feel guilty in our society for getting sick, as though disease is evidence we are doing something wrong. And perhaps we are, but I don't believe that blaming ourselves for our illnesses is conducive to either prevention or healing. When I would tell Dad about my medical issues, he'd say the doctor was wrong. If I managed to convince him, he'd say don't tell your mother. Dad wasn't nearly as adept at soothing our anxieties as he was at provoking them and without a mother to soften life's blows, I had to buck up as they had wished.

Caring for Mom and protecting her from stress became my role in our relationship which, in some ways, helped me to grow stronger in my own capabilities. The consequence, however, was the evolvement of a very durable savior complex which when Dad died, shot into action faster than I could unwind.

I asked Mom to live near me so that I could care for her.

In truth I never expected she'd take me up on it, she being barely able to decide what to eat let alone move across the country. When she stunned me with her agreement, I felt both excitement and panic. Did my mother actually want to be near me? I couldn't wrap my head around it. We were at odds my entire life. She saw me as the pot-stirrer, an inconvenient mirror to everything in her that she wanted to hide. We always started out in a blissful reunion but in three days time we'd revert back to our old and stubborn roles. We couldn't hold any connection beyond that and her delight in seeing me dried up like a flower in the desert.

But she said yes. Maybe she liked me after all. I always knew Mom loved me but never that she liked who I was. And her love was the kind of love that kept me handcuffed and silenced instead of lifted and encouraged. There was a sense of death in it. In fact she would often declare her love by saying, "I would lay down and die for you kids," to which I silently retorted "But will you stand up and live?"

While the adult in me knew all of this too well, the child in me celebrated her long-awaited wish for a mother who actually wanted her. "History be gone," she cried, adorning my skeptical eyes with ridiculously rose-colored glasses. I shut myself off from the reality that would await us if we actually carried out this plan. Nothing had changed and certainly nothing would change in her moving to Arizona. Yet, out I went, in absolute merriment, in search of a home for her and her sister. I was only minimally sobered by all of the requirements and conditions she placed on her coming.

The quid pro quo's were reminiscent of our kitchen table contract forty years prior. If I wanted Mom I would need an escrow account of entertainment vouchers, as she "needed" to go out to dinner three nights a week, have card nights, and movie outings. In her peculiar bird way she never demanded I be responsible for her social, psychological, and physical well-being, but nonetheless it would in fact all be up to me. If I failed in any of it and Mom was unhappy at any time, it would be my fault. With minimal pushback I agreed to all of it, knowing full well the implausibility of my success.

We found a perfect home four blocks away from mine, meeting all of their needs. We showed them videos and they acted pleased, which surprised me. One was fussier than the other, and it was unlikely that the first place I showed them would be adequate. I was sure their frozen smiles weren't actual approval but chose not to question it. As they prepared for the move, I sat in front of their new home in my car, dreaming silly fantasies. I allowed hope to rise in my chest, until a moment of reality snuck up, showing me a sliver of our inevitable future, of a time I would sit in front of this same home, staring at where my mother once lived, now gone, and my heart broken. I would be the one seeing her out of this life. Could I bear that journey? I wondered. I told myself it didn't matter, it was meant to be, all predetermined in some spacious void. Throughout my childhood I was the one who slept on the floor by her bed when she cried out in pain from debilitating endometriosis, I carried her to the bathroom with endless bouts of stomach attacks, and I was the child she believed would save her from the grief of her dead mother. It would come full circle now, and we would be brought back to the beginning. I was my mother's first caretaker in our family, and now I would be her last. I couldn't rationally explain why I was making a decision to reunite with a mother who had caused me so much pain, so I created a transcendent fantasy to ease my mind.

When Mom and her sister arrived there wasn't a honeymoon period to speak of. It was never the joyous occasion I had built in my mind but rather a surrender to their sad reality. I was the lesser of two evils, my competitor an assisted-living facility. I felt their ambivalence lurking in every corner of the house. The house, it turned out, they never really liked. Mom hated the color of the paint, Anne deemed the exterior ugly. Mom detested the fireplace and had me buy a screen to hide its sooty appearance. The brand new wood plank floors looked dirty to her and she complained about a weird smell coming from the vents.

The air around them felt heavy, laden with loss. Anne made it known from the start this was not her choice and she reminded me at every opportunity. Her commitment to misery and dissatisfaction was relentless, as was her determination to keep me from ever feeling useful. I would forever fall short and that would be my punishment for making her share my mother.

Resentments mounted. Caregiving seemed both futile and endless. At least when you care for children you have adult authority and control, or at the very least the illusion of such. Taking care of Mom and Anne was a daily battle of wills. They were completely dependent on me and yet insistent on maintaining whatever control they had left. Mom refused to drink water despite now living in the desert and she was constantly dehydrated, suffering headaches, stomach ailments, and vertigo. I measured out her daily required intake, flavored the water and pled for her to drink. She resisted like a pouty child, drinking less than four ounces a day. Anne refused at-home care, expecting me to miss work to chauffeur her to appointments. We battled.

As I had anticipated, they pressured me for entertainment, wanting to go to movies, on vacations, to play cards. When a night spent together was over, they guilted me for leaving so early. It was never enough. I adored the playful times with Mom, rarely having had them as a child but the mix of pleasure and obligation sat like curdled milk in my stomach. I often went home feeling sick and drained.

Three years passed, of living in two worlds, a foot in my life and the rest of my body in theirs, when Anne suffered a sudden brain hemorrhage. She was ninety-three years old and had survived a bad heart for decades, but her body finally succumbed. We had played cards and drank her favorite nonalcoholic beer the night before. She showed no signs of illness. The stroke was massive and recovery impossible. In the hospital we sat with her awaiting her last breath and when the nurse finally shook her head confirming her passing, Mom wailed and began climbing into Anne's bed. The nurse, also in tears, helped me contain Mom as she released guttural sobs, "Anne, do you want me to come with you?", in an even more intimate expression of grief than at my father's funeral. The nurse assured Mom she had plenty of loved ones who needed her but I knew it was over. When Dad had passed, a know-it-all nurse told me Mom would soon be next, as that's how old people die. Correcting her ignorance, I informed her it was her sister who she would someday follow.

Mom never went back to her own house after Anne died. She moved in with us without any of us ever making an actual decision to do so. She simply stayed and eventually we began moving her stuff a little at a time. Each day was a challenge. Her heart was broken. She didn't want to live without her family. That's how she said it.

"I have no one left," she whispered one day, "my family is all gone now." And when she looked up at my face, she seemed startled and quickly added, "Well, I have you kids of course, but I mean my family is gone"

"I am your family Mom."

"Well, not my actual family."

"Come again?"

"You are my extended family."

"Your extended family? Me and my sister and my brother are your extended family?"

"Yes."

"The children you gave birth to? That came from your body? Are your extended family?"

"Yes."

"Are you your mother's family?"

"Of course."

"But wouldn't you be her extended family? Wouldn't her sisters and brothers be her actual family?"

"No."

"So you are everyone's family and I am no one's?"

Pausing a moment, she looked at me pitifully. "Well, because you don't have children."

If it was just a matter of words, I might have dismissed them as more of Mom's nonsensical logic, but the reality behind the words was real for me. It mirrored my experience. I didn't feel like Mom's family, not like children do. She designated herself as the maid and that is often what she felt like to us, a nanny of sorts. She didn't spend her days wanting to know what we needed, who we were, what we believed, or who we wanted to be. She spent them cleaning up after us. That was the extent of her role as she saw it. In my first session with my therapist some fifteen years ago, I told her what I wanted more than anything else in life was to be claimed. I didn't know where the word came from but I suspect it had been lying around my psyche for a while. Each of us in this world desires claiming, to be part of, connected, attached, owned, and possessed in a way that makes us feel of value and worthy of protection. "She is mine," touches a primal chord in children, it is fundamental. For Mom to say I am not her family puts it in a realistic light. I was not hers, but rather an extended line, a secondary connection, after that of her siblings, particularly her sister. It gave her permission to love her more.

Mom's sister was the love of her life. I realize how that sounds and yet there's no other way to say it. Dad couldn't compete any more than the rest of us. She owned Mom's heart. Of course it wasn't a physical relationship but it was an intimate one. They were fused. Dad used to joke that he got two wives for the price of one, but sharing Mom was painful for him. It hurt all of us.

Realizing that I desired claiming made it possible. When you know what to look for you will find it. While prior relationships were positive and wonderful in their own ways it wasn't until I met Lisa that I finally felt that claiming. I am first in all things in her life, and I am her real family, as she is mine.

In therapy we can usually boil it down the same way for clients. When they are not being claimed in their relationships they experience a lot of heartache and pain. When we explore their relationship wounds it often comes down to their partner's lack of prioritizing them. "He was working while I was giving birth," "She never takes my side," it's things like that that hurt us at our core. If a relationship doesn't meet that fundamental need, it's likely not the right one.

Chapter 22
Full Circle

*"Life is a full circle, widening until it joins
the circle motions of the infinite." —Anais Nin*

The old wounds always found a way to the surface
without either of us directly raising them. They slipped
through the cracks of Mom's repression. She needed to talk
about them, to rectify them finally, but once they hit the light
of day they were quickly eclipsed by her denials. She had
witnessed so much of my father's abuse of us, but shielded
herself from the reality of it. Despite this, she'd bring up
subjects certain to provoke. The unconscious mind is more
stubborn than even Mom's compulsions, it wants what it
wants and forces the conflict to the surface like an ocean
boom brings up the drowned. She often poked at me about
the pedophile uncle, telling me how she cooked for him,
cleaned his bathroom, made my father take him to doctors
appointments—knowing full well it salted my wounds.
There were times when she catered to him at my expense
and subduing my reactions was simply too difficult. When
it came to Dad, it was always an effort to rewrite history, to

convince herself that she had heroically protected us from his rage. Sometimes she would talk about abuse in other families as though negatively comparing them to ours, making us a delusional exception to the dysfunction out in the world.

It was yet another argument about the past. Her story versus my story, her scrubbed memory versus my stubborn one. This one was different but I hadn't realized at the time just how different. Her memory edged even more into denial but with a more irrational twist than usual. It was a new narrative and more bizarre.

"I just can't see how a parent can hit a child," she said after watching a bad movie of the week.

"Yep, awful." I can usually bear about three pokes before reacting and I'm working really hard at not taking the bait.

"I always told your father, just talk to them, they listen to you."

"Right."

She is awaiting my typical reaction but I'm counting to ten in my head, stalling an outburst. She seems disappointed, "Well, I guess some families have real problems."

"Sure enough."

She finally pulls the trigger, aiming directly into my heart,

"You know your father always had such a bad temper but I never let him do that to you kids."

"Ok Mom, enough, please, let's not do this again."

"Do what? I don't know what you're talking about."

"Please stop with the denials. You know perfectly well what Dad did to us. Why can't you just admit it already. Better yet, say you're sorry that it happened so we can be done with it for Christ's sake."

"What should I be sorry for? What did I do?"

"It's not what you did Mom, it's what you didn't do." She looked puzzled. "You didn't stop him, and in fact, you provoked him."

"What do you mean? When did he ever hit any of you?" she looked genuinely confused.

"Well, which time do you want me to remind you of now? How about when Donna came home late and he threw her at the wall like a rag doll? We both thought he'd kill her that night. He was insane, I even jumped on his back and had him in a choke hold."

"I don't remember that all at."

"Right, it's all fake news Mom."

"Well, I don't know what I was supposed to do if it was late. Was I supposed to get out of bed?"

I stared at her, my turn to be bewildered. "What!"

"What?"

"You didn't want to get out of bed to stop him from beating her?"

"Well, if it was late…"

Mom never slept much, she wasn't in bed that night, she was right in the middle of it all. This new denial baffled me.

"See it never goes anywhere, this argument is senseless. When are we going to quit chasing it around in circles? I don't know why I even bother reacting except that I can't no matter how hard I try," I say.

"Well, I don't want to be a bother to you."

"That's not what I mean."

"I think you regret me moving here" she says. This her go-to whenever she wants reassurance that she is wanted and loved and not a burden. I give it to her every time, whether it's true or not I tell her I have no regrets. But on this day I can't manage a simple denial and shrug my shoulders in an easily interpreted agreement, a yes to her suspicion. This takes her aback, eyes wide in disbelief.

"So you do regret having me to come to Arizona?"

I shrug again adding a raised brow this time, completely indifferent to her pain.

"Fine," she says, "then I'll get out of your way."

"You're not in my way Mom," I say through a clenched jaw.

"Well, clearly I am, and I don't feel well now, I'm going to take my pill and lie down."

As I chased Mom around this merry-go-round, my mother-in-law Vera lay in a hospital bed dying. I resented my own mother's neediness in a cruel comparison to Vera's genuinely tragic life. If anyone deserved to be taken in and cared for it was she. She had made real sacrifices for her family, not the martyred fantasies of Mom's. I was embarrassed by the conspicuous inequities of their fortunes.

Mom was eighty-eight years old, and had never spent so much as a single night alone. Vera had lost two husbands before she was fifty, had worked to feed her family on her own, cared for her own mentally ill mother, and was the fiercest protector of her family I had ever known.

"We're heading out to the hospital Mom, do you need anything before I go?" "How's Vera?"

Our moms hadn't exactly become friends over the thirty years of being in-laws, as Mom really didn't have friends and besides she wasn't exactly the kind of friend Vera would choose. Our mothers couldn't be more different as though from different generations although only five years apart. My mother seemed ancient in her ways when compared to Vera who always kept up with the latest everything, until she had an aneurysm at fifty-nine years old. Following three craniotomies, her brain injury had made her more in line with Mom's incapacity to think in any real depth and as both entered their eighties they were closer in functioning and thus closer allies.

"Not good Mom, doctors say any time now."

"I'm so sorry, please send her my love, that poor woman."

"I know, it's been awful."

"Lucky" she says, smirking.

"What?"

"Lucky, your T-shirt says Lucky." She says this as though winning an argument.

I look down at my shirt and roll my eyes, "Whatever."

"I want to take a shower. Do you think it's okay? I know you don't like me to do it when you're not home but I'm very careful."

I alway argue and win this point with her, today I don't have the emotional capital to try. "Whatever you think best Mom, you're an adult."

"Ok, well, I guess I'll wait. You won't be late?"

"I shouldn't be."

When we get to the hospital Vera is shockingly sitting up in a chair. She smiles when she sees us coming through the door. We are disoriented by the contradiction from yesterday to today. We had come to say goodbye and instead we were greeted with an unimaginable hello. She is coherent, alert, and making jokes, and we are in utter disbelief.

At the end of our visit as we go to leave she calls my name, "Juli!" she shouts.

I turn around and walk back to stand over her bed. She pulls my hand into her hers, her eyes drilling into me.

"You know your mother loves you," she says. I furrow my brow in question.

"Your mother, she loves you very much. Always remember that."

"Okay," I say, intent on appeasing her.

"Okay, good," she says.

On the way home I call Mom to let her know we are on our way. The call goes to voice mail. I leave a message, "You must be in the shower," I chide, "you couldn't wait could you? I'll be home in about twenty minutes."

When we get home Mom's bathroom door is closed, so I take the dogs out and then go into my own bathroom. I'm not certain but I think I hear noises coming through the adjoining wall, so I try to listen. Initially I can't make them out but suddenly I realize they are moans, and my heart sinks so fast I don't feel it drop, only smashing to bottom. I run to her door, but it's locked. I bang on it in terror and hear my mother trying to cry for help but the sounds are muffled, grunting like I've never heard. I bang harder on the door as though it will open from my sheer will as I scream for Lisa. I turn the knob with all my might and stunningly it opens to the sight of my ninety-pound mother, wrapped in a towel, laying on the floor making feral sounds. I drop to my knees and hold her head in my hands. I see a gash on her face, another on her leg, and her tongue is hanging to the left side. The information computes in flashes of understanding. Fall. Hit head. Brain injury. No. Tongue. Stroke. Stroke. Stroke. I scream inside, No No No No No.

Lisa says an ambulance is on the way. I hold Mom's head, as she tries to speak but can't. She is looking at me with one eye, the other off to the side. She is trying to get up but can't. She is trying to cover her naked body with the towel, self-conscious even in this state. I cradle her and tell her, "I have you, it's going to be okay, I'll take care of you Mom," but her one eye begins to close, as though now able to rest. I'm holding her head and reality is pushing in against my will, "Please," I pray to who ever is listening, "please not yet, not like this," and then to Mom, "I am so sorry, Mom,

I'm so, so sorry. I didn't mean it, I don't have regrets Mom, I never had regrets, I'm so sorry Mom, I love you. I am so, so sorry," but she can't open her eyes, or won't.

We follow the ambulance to the hospital. They leave us in the waiting room, not allowing us to see her. I know what that means, I know what to expect, but still I hope. The admitting doctor finally calls us into a private room, squelching my last hope. He tells us she is never going home, that the mother I knew is no longer, and if I wanted what was best for her I would let her go without aggressive intervention. Saving her would cause only suffering. When he's done I release every bit of restrained grief, pain, and fear, and sob into my hands. When there are no tears left to cry I look up at the doctor. He waits, he understands, he is silent.

"Can upset or stress from a fight have caused this?" I ask like a guilty child. "No." he says firmly, gently, reassuringly. I hear him, I want to believe him, but inside I know otherwise. I killed my mother. I made her feel like a burden, her very worst fear, and now she's going to die. She wanted to die. She always said she'd rather be dead than be a burden and now she was going to die believing it.

Two days later, we took Mom off life support and went home just before midnight. I walked into a moonlit backyard to breathe. At my feet was a tiny bird, struggling to free its bloodied wings from the ground. I reached for a tissue and wrapped him inside, watching as he takes his last breath. For the next ten days I find one dead bird after another. There was one our dog caught, one that hit the window, one on the walkway, another under our orange tree. I thought maybe a neighbor had put rat poison out, but then I started seeing them in my travels. The last one I saw hit my car. It was Mom, I concluded, letting me know I killed her.

It went on like this for months after, my constant searching for proof that I was responsible for her death and a monstrous daughter. I couldn't reason myself out of the grief, nor could I use any of the counseling experience I had acquired over the years. I was inside of it, looking out, and all I saw was Mom's crushing disappointment staring back at me. I did not dream of her, nor did I feel like she was still with me. It felt cold and stark and vacant. She had left me and was glad to be free.

Apathetic is one of those words that pulls apart perfectly. Being apathetic makes me feels like a pathetic being. Feeling too much is uncomfortable; not feeling enough is deadening. Mom's death felt both too close and too far away. I would cry spontaneously, yet my body felt numb and detached. I wanted to feel more connected to my pain but it wasn't how I felt. Week after week I'd attempt to work it out in therapy.

"Why don't I feel more?" I'd ask repeatedly until Renee, my analyst, would squirm in her seat. I had been seeing her for more than a decade, as I am a firm believer in Freud's guidance that "you can only take your patient as far as you have been yourself."

Renee's eyes have this way of glazing over when I'm off track, fatigued by my constant rerouting away from emotional pain. Like medical doctors, we are the worst patients, often trying to lead and do our own analysis, impatient with another perspective. It is hard for me to entertain her points.

"Can you allow yourself your experience?" she asks.

I ignore.

"Without judgment?"

"Apparently not."

My lack of feeling must confirm that I am the monster Mom accused me of being: emotionally blocked and lacking compassion. A pathetic. It's a strange juxtaposition to be overwhelmed and numb. I can't decide which way to judge myself and who is right.

"You have had complicated feelings for your mother your entire life. Why do you think it unusual to have a complicated grief?" she wants to know.

"What kind of person doesn't miss their mother after she dies? It's not like I didn't love her. I adored her. Every day I'd come home and go right into her room to see her. I loved taking care of her. Why don't I miss her?"

She shifts in her recliner again and pulls the black shawl from the ottoman onto her legs. She is quiet. I hate when she does this. She gives me room to drown.

"I loved her so much."

She nods, eyes softened.

"I want to feel. I want to grieve, I want to fucking miss her," I cry.

We sit silently.

"Juli, why do you think you're feeling so blocked?"

"Maybe because of my guilt."

"Because of the fight you had before she died."

I can't look at her. With my head down I nod.

She nods as well and waits.

"Did you ever consider that maybe you were supposed to have that difficult conversation? That maybe you and your mother finally had an authentic exchange instead of the usual avoidant defenses and charade you both played?" She waits for an answer but I don't have one.

"Think about it. You know the reality was painful and ugly. You can't cherry-pick it, it was what it was. Yes, you hurt her and she hurt you too—very much so. You weren't the bad guy, you had a relationship and that's what happens. You finally got to speak your truth, by not acquiescing to her manipulation for reassurance and love you set the boundary and while that is painful and dark, it's life. It finally got real between the two of you and maybe that's what she came for all along. A final resolution of reality for you both, it was what it was."

The words hang in the air, and I am unsure I want to let them in. What will they do to me if I allow this to be true? My mind debates it but my body feels a resonance with them. I always believed Mom and I were fated for a psychic entanglement. It had to be. She birthed me into her conflict and we sparred an entire lifetime. I fueled the sparks unlike anyone else in our family. I couldn't resist the bait. When I stop to really allow it to unfold I see the full circle of our relationship.

Just as her mother had died in her arms, from a massive stroke, on her bathroom floor—my mother left me in my arms, from a massive stroke, on my bathroom floor. I came into this world as an answer to her grief and I had always been for her the bond to both her mother and her pain. She would leave me this way to show me the incarnation of that bond as well at its expiration. We had completed the circle.

When I accept the darkness that lives in all of us, I can calm it. When I let in the fullness of the human condition, I can join its collective experience. When I accept that we are all fated for heartbreakingly difficult influences on each other, that it is our inevitable job on earth to hurt and be hurt, to fight and to repair, to find the truth behind our masks and still to love all that we are and are not, then I can be free of the despair of imperfection. This is the second full circle of Mom and me. She died unable to free herself from her internal, futile war and maybe she wanted me to find peace with my own. Mom reflected my shadowed need for perfection, and witnessing it all these years, hating it and wishing it away, was the core of my work. It was a constant reminder of my own anger at that part of myself that mirrored her compulsions, needing always to be clean, and pure, and innocent—in essence being half a human being. In her death, the mirror is foggy. I am not sure of the direction without being mad at her compulsions, but in the work, in having a real and unabashed look at myself, I am finding my own way.

It has been nearly three years since Mom has gone. The journey has been unrelenting and revealing. I still see Mom on the floor of my bathroom every now and again, forcing me to close my eyes and remind myself it is not happening now, that in the present moment there is no pain. It took nearly a year for the guilt of that last fight to start dissipating and I credit time, as much as therapy for that. Talking always helps, but time is a necessary variable. All things fade, good and bad. Now as I see my partner deal with similar regrets as her mom has passed as well, I know that hers will inevitably fall into the background too.

The concept of predestined fates helps keep the painful stuff in context. Believing that everything has a purpose makes the hard times bearable, as they are the rain for the trees. It all grows. As I was writing the ending to this book Mom came to me for the first time, in the middle of the night. Not in a vision, like she claimed to have happened with her mother, but rather in an unnamable way. The best I can describe it is that I felt her essence, beyond the five senses.

I still can't decide the nature of our connection. There are so many more steps in front of me. I am a toddler pulling myself up on the coffee table as there is so much more work to do on my relationship with Mom, even in death. When Renee has me consider that Mom truly loved and wanted to be with me, I am genuinely brought to tears in disbelief. I cannot hold the notion in any real way, as though it comes in and my brain banishes it back out. It is so hard to reconcile that she loved me through her mental illness when so much of our time together felt rejecting. I have, over the course of my lifetime, reduced myself to being the burden she projected onto me. In last week's session, when I tried to stay with the feeling of her love for me I broke down and broke through another inch of resistance. And so it goes.

Her absence in my life, emotionally before and physically now, is still hard, but as I approach the end of my fifth decade in life, I turn more to myself. I am no longer drawn to dependencies like that of Ms. M, or her many subsequent replacements. I am the mom now, and pretty capable most of the time. Staying attuned to my own needs continues to be challenging. I forget nearly every time to stop and pause and check in with myself. When I do stop to notice, I try to be the mirroring parent and not laugh at my own pain, or debate and invalidate. And when I replace judgment with curiosity, compassion is the frequent outcome. I suggest my clients equate viewing their emotions like you would view cells on a microscope slide. Scientists don't judge appearance or activity, but rather observe with immense curiosity, wanting to learn versus critique. We don't need to emotionally react to our emotions as much as we need to sit patiently by. Always remember to resist that dreaded second arrow!

Quite unexpectedly I have rediscovered my ten-year-old self since Mom's passing, that person who existed before all the scars starting piling up. During the Covid lockdowns in fact, she went wild creating, bringing to life so much passion that had been lost over the years.

Free from our caregiving roles, my partner and I have since moved to the Oregon Coast where I feel closer to that inner kid than ever before. I so appreciate her now. Her rambunctiousness had been pushed so hard into the shadows as it threatened Mom's sense of safety, but she's out there now, feeling quite cocky. It's a good feeling.

My gnat-like minions do visit on a daily basis demanding order and perfection. I want to shoo them away like the annoyances they are yet they are vital to my well-being. The problems don't really ever change, just our reactions to them, and that's okay. They are the reminders that some things are amiss, so I have learned to use them positively. I take their warning flares seriously. They are here for a reason. They are alerting me to my neglected fears and wounds, ones that I fail to see or address. It's annoying to need them, the obsessions and compulsions, and not know my needs without their nudging, but it just means the work happens retroactively which is also okay. Yesterday the seams of the lamp shades made me crazed, as did the twisted Christmas stockings on the mantel. I waited until bedtime to sneak in my corrections. While lying in bed, sleep not nearing, I ask the minions—the psyche's soldiers—what they want. They have a laundry list.

"Right," I surrender, "you always know, but if I promise to do my work, can I still turn the seams to the back where they belong?"

The answer is,

Yes.

EPILOGUE
Coming Home to Ourselves

I've discussed the concept of projection throughout this book and hope you've gotten a good understanding of its nature and function. We all use projections because we all have psyches in need of balance and healing. If we were able to handle the repressed realities of our lives, projections wouldn't exist. They are helpful and necessary for a period of time. Eventually we need to identify and expose them as they linger dysfunctionally, in essence an old key to a new lock.

The easiest way to catch a projection is to watch our reactions to otherwise inconsequential things such as how others look, their successes or failures, their intelligence or ignorance, and the like. These are things that rarely affect us personally and are often none of our business but we have strong reactions and opinions nonetheless. Why do they cause such deep emotional disturbances in us when they are irrelevant to our lives? Psychologists believe that while they don't impact our conscious realities they incite our repressed and unconscious conflicts.

I often ask my patients to rate their reactions against the importance of the things they are reacting to and if there is a large gap between them, they are likely projecting. For example, my favorite place to project is in politics. I will generally get a knee-jerk reaction to both sides of the fence, with one party feeling too aggressive and one feeling too passive, which represents the ultimate conflict in my house growing up, whittled down to its barest nub. At the end of the day, politicians need not occupy any space in my head or my heart and yet I will experience feelings of deep anger and fear nonetheless. It's the internalization of both my parents' coping systems, which has become my internal battle between my own passivity and aggressiveness.

Another good way of checking in with our unconscious mechanisms is to rate our reactions in our relationships. If my partner did that thing again that annoys me, I need to identify where the offense lies in terms of importance, with one being the most innocuous and ten being the most hurtful, and then measure that against my reaction with one being a modest annoyance and ten being a Tasmanian devil. If I find myself spinning out over mild infractions I need to sit my butt on the zabuton for a bit and practice the RAIN meditation.

Let's say my partner forgot my request to pick up something at the grocery store and instead of patiently reminding her, I blame and shame her for being so thoughtless. The infraction is rated a one, as it is as far a cry from things such as abuse, betrayal, and infidelity as it can be. My reaction however is a six in that it made me moderately angry. The place that lies between the one and the six is where my conflict resides. Beneath the anger I am feeling unloved, unseen, and neglected. When I practice the RAIN meditation I see that those are the familiar feelings I have, ones that are rooted in my childhood and that while Lisa may have forgotten my yogurt she still loves and prioritizes me.

Remember, practicing the R in RAIN is recognizing the feelings—unloved, unseen, neglected, angry, resentful, etc. The A represents the Allowing of those feelings, in that we make space and room for them in our bodies and minds with an open and nonjudgmental heart. It is okay I feel these feelings, they are not bad or wrong or childish but simply my being human. I send "yes" energy to my body as it releases and expands, versus "no" energy that would squeeze and contract. I breathe into the feelings reassuring myself I will be okay, that emotions are tolerable when we work with them in this way. The I represents Investigate and during this part I allow myself to consider what might be beneath the reaction, such as old wounds or current stressors. In this example, I see that these are the same feelings I often had as a child when my parents neglected my needs—and to the child now, I can enter into the N or Nurture stage of the meditation and send care and validation with a hand over my heart.

Over the course of my career I have seen that it is in the stories we tell ourselves that so much pain is derived—the second arrow. We don't have a choice in terms of pain, life is going to bring us plenty. However, we can choose our

279

reactions to pain in the stories we spin. In time and with a whole lot of practice we control the narrative. Our go-to reaction needs to become one of self-love, non-judgment, and compassion. For those of us who have had difficult childhoods it may require breaking through the shame. Self-admonishment is often reflexive so we need to have a positive affirmation as the last word in our self-talk, ensuring that the last entry into the program is a compassionate one, as it will run the show.

Lastly, I encourage you, my reader, to talk and share your story with a trusted listener as the one thing that shame cannot trump is our shared love and acceptance of each other, just as we are. Shame thrives on silence, like a violent domestic relationship, keeping us isolated in our stories and cut off from outside perspectives. When we communicate and express our wounds they will initially hurt upon opening, but then gradually take in the morning dew, to grow and blossom into the beauty of our experiences.

I'll leave off with Rumi's poem that I hope will inspire you on your own journey.

The Guest House

This being human is a guest house.
Every morning a new arrival.
A joy, a depression, a meanness,
some momentary awareness comes
as an unexpected visitor.
Welcome and entertain them all!
Even if they're a crowd of sorrows,
who violently sweep your house
empty of its furniture,
still, treat each guest honorably.
He may be clearing you out
for some new delight.
The dark thought, the shame, the malice,
meet them at the door laughing,
and invite them in.
Be grateful for whoever comes,
because each has been sent
as a guide from beyond.

Stay safe and well.

GPSIA information can be obtained
at www.ICGtesting.com
Printed in the USA
LVHW111635040822
725105LV00020B/162